So Here We Are

Also by David Caddy

Poetry
The Balance (1981)
Anger (1982)
The Beating on the Door (1987)
Honesty (1990)
Continuity (1995)
Desire (1997)
The Willy Poems (2004)
Man in Black (2007)
The Bunny Poems (2011)

Literature
London: City of Words (with Westrow Cooper, 2006)

So Here We Are

David Caddy

Shearsman Books

First published in the United Kingdom 2012 by
Shearsman Books Ltd
50 Westons Hill Drive
Emersons Green
BRISTOL
BS16 7DF

Shearsman Books Ltd Registered Office
30–31 St. James Place, Mangotsfield, Bristol BS16 9JB
(this address not for correspondence)

ISBN 978-1-84861-091-0
First Edition

Copyright © David Caddy, 2009, 2012.

The right of David Caddy to be identified as the author of this work
has been asserted by him in accordance with the
Copyrights, Designs and Patents Act of 1988.
All rights reserved.

Acknowledgements
I would like to thank Didi Menendez, without whom these essays would not have
been written, Luc Simonic, for introducing me to Didi, and Pris Campbell,
for her technical support.

I must thank Ian Brinton, Brian Hinton, Ketaki Kushari Dyson,
Edward Field, Sarah Hopkins, John Kinsella and Nathaniel Tarn
for their enthusiastic support of these essays.
Finally, I must thank Tony Frazer for his efforts
in the smooth publication of this book.

The essay on Jeremy Prynne was subsequently revised and published as
'Notes Towards a Preliminary Reading of J.H. Prynne's *Poems*' in *A Manner of
Utterance: The Poetry of J.H. Prynne*, edited by Ian Brinton (Shearsman 2009).

Contents

Introduction		7
Letter 1:	Ralegh	9
Letter 2:	Barnes and the English Poetry Canon	17
Letter 3:	Sonia Orwell: The Venus of Euston Road	25
Letter 4:	Blake's Marriage	34
Letter 5:	Ethnopoetics	43
Letter 6:	Salisbury	50
Letter 7:	Bill Griffiths	59
Letter 8:	In Praise of Walking	66
Letter 9:	Allen Fisher's *Place*	73
Letter 10:	Bunting and Fitzrovia	80
Letter 11:	Tom Raworth's Comedy	88
Letter 12:	Poetry and Celebrity	96
Letter 13:	John Kinsella's Anti-Pastoral	106
Letter 14:	J.H. Prynne	114
Letter 15:	Andrew Crozier	124
Letter 16:	John Riley	132
Letter 17:	David Gascoyne	139
Letter 18:	Forests	146

Introduction

In April 2007, when Didi Menendez, publishing director of MiPO publications and miPOradio, invited me to present a monthly series of literary talks, my remit was to be personal, direct and contemporary, in the manner of Alistair Cooke's *Letters from America*. *So Here We Are: Poetic Letters from England* began somewhat gingerly on 7 May 2007, with an essay on aspects of my poetic background, and picked up pace from there. I attempted to give some background to the contemporary poetry scene in England as well as responding to the deaths of poets, such as Bill Griffiths and Andrew Crozier. The talks were written quickly and intended as intelligent introductions rather than definitive statements. Their aim was to stimulate the reader/listener and prompt further reading and discussion.

So Here We Are soon found a loyal and expanding internet audience. Some of the audio podcasts were downloaded by several thousand people; others by eight hundred or so. It was the vision and diligence of Didi Menendez that made this programme such a success. She found a considerable number of internet outlets for the audio podcasts beyond miPOradio and my blog at davidcaddy.blogspot.com. Many friends not only listened to the podcasts but added links to their websites or blogs and in this way *So Here We Are* found its place on the internet. Such generosity of spirit is enlivening.

Letter 1: Ralegh

I should say that I love both English and American poetry and that I read both in equal measure and delight. I suppose that that already marks my card as a figure concerned with what might be usefully called the melting pot of Anglo-American poetry and poetics. In England there is great hostility from the poetry establishment and the mainstream towards Anglo-American poetry, not to mention modernist and postmodernist developments.

In this sense, by my very interest, I am an English outsider. Indeed I have been called the outsider's insider and I do like to challenge accepted versions of literary history. Given this position, I may be able to shed light on aspects of English poetry, Anglo-American poetry and the state of the art. Having said that, we all have our prejudices and I shall be trying to curb mine. I rather like the idea of being a reporter from the frontline, an Alistair Cooke producing a poetic letter from England. *So Here We Are.*

To start with, in this first letter or two, I want to talk about my poetic heritage, the one that impacted during my childhood and beyond, and hopefully through this approach reveal some things that are peculiarly English.

I have lived most of my life in tiny villages and towns in rural North Dorset, which is situated in central southern England, and some twenty-five miles inland from the Jurassic coast, as it now called by those eager to drum up tourist trade, and some thirty miles south-west of Stonehenge, the Neolithic and Bronze age megalithic monument.

I live in an ancient landscape where the past looks at you from every angle. I look out of my study window at wild deer grazing and at the Neolithic hill fort, Hod Hill, with its visible Roman settlement from the first century AD. In England you feel you are part of the long march of everyman.

When I went to Sturminster Newton primary school, the first poetry that I can recall hearing and reading after nursery rhymes, hymns and folk ballads were the poems and songs of William Shakespeare.

> When icicles hang by the wall
> And Dick the shepherd blows his nail
> And Tom bears logs into the hall
> And milk comes frozen home in pail.[1]

Letter 1: Ralegh

This comes from the end of the play *Love's Labour's Lost* and I suspect my teacher thought that this was suitable for us country boys and girls.

Coming from a family where there were no books and no one had ever gone to University, I resisted such things. I recall complaining about the irrelevance of such old writing and saying that I would never become a poet. However, I was crestfallen at not being selected ever to appear in any school production or sports team. I felt excluded and was. I was surely as good as the others. I loved that magical school play, *A Midsummer Night's Dream,* which I could only watch but not be part of. Access to the heritage is closely guarded and if you can find a way in to this, it may not be easy.

I think we may have read some of the *Sonnets* but cannot remember for certain. I was a dreamer, looking out of the window. I was also a playground fighter, hitting back hard at the bullies, trying to be left alone. I am more certain that we read *The Passionate Pilgrim* poems VII and VIII:

> Fair is my love, but not so fair as fickle
> Mild as a dove, but neither true nor trusty
> Brighter than glass, and yet, as glass is, brittle
> Softer than wax, and yet, as iron, rusty:[2]

Shakespeare was standard fare for eleven-year-olds at the time. I did know creative writing and, when it came to the age 11-plus examinations, I recall writing a story (a *composition*) where the characters were subordinate to the detail and structure and the end was the same as the beginning. I certainly had no idea of the *Nouveau Roman* at that time and I rather suspect that neither did my examiner, for I failed my 11-plus exam and was confined not to the local Grammar School but to the Secondary Modern, a school designed to produce farm workers and, more secretly, I suspect, poets.

The school was divided into Houses named after local poets: Ralegh, Barnes, Young and Hardy. Walter Ralegh (1552–1618), William Barnes (1801–1886), the dialect poet, Robert Young (1811–1908) and Thomas Hardy (1840–1926) were the forces for which we applied ourselves. Old people in Stur had known both Young and Hardy.

The Hardy Players had brought his plays to the town for years. My friend, Jean Guy, lived in the farmhouse at nearby Bagber where Barnes had been born. The old School House where he had gone to school was now being used by the primary school as a dining room. Hardy had written poems, such as 'Overlooking The River Stour' and 'On Sturminster Footbridge' and the novel, *The Return of the Native*, when he lived at Sturminster Newton in 1877.[3] Poets permeated the town.

Although I will mostly be talking about Ralegh, I am going to take a brief detour.

In December 2005, Thomas Hardy's poem 'On Sturminster Bridge'[4] was widely used as part of a local protest against the development of a large house that altered the historic Sturminster Mill view. It was published in national newspapers along with photos of the Mill and proposed building plans that had been passed by bare quorum of local councillors on quiet night. The house is currently on the market at a cost of one million pounds (ca. $1.6 million). The local artists, musicians, writers and councillors who protested felt that it was an eyesore development, planned by people who had no regard for the historic Mill view. The water mill is mentioned in the *Domesday Book* of 1086, that great survey of England made by order of William the Conqueror, and could well have been painted by John Constable when he travelled through Sturminster Newton from Salisbury on the way to Lyme Regis, on the Dorset coast, in 1821.

Such poetic protests are not uncommon. The Northern Irish poet, Seamus Heaney, is currently involved in trying to prevent a dual carriageway being built through the wetlands of South Derry, where he grew up, and about which he has written so eloquently. William Barnes prevented a railway cutting through both the heart of Dorchester and Maiden Castle by leading a poetic protest in 1845–6.

Ralegh was a dashing gentleman poet, soldier and explorer, born in Devon, and a Dorset man by choice. His relationship with Queen Elizabeth is the subject of the film, *The Golden Age*, due out this autumn.[5] Cate Blanchett plays Elizabeth, Clive Owen, Ralegh, Geoffrey Rush, Walsingham and Samantha Morton, Mary Queen of Scots. Doubtless you will see Ralegh etch with a diamond "Fain would I climb, yet fear

Letter 1: Ralegh

I to fall" on a Court windowpane and Elizabeth reply, "If thy heart fails thee, climb not at all".

Ralegh was a poetic role-player. His friend, Edmund Spenser, said that he was "the sommers Nightingale", writing poetry of "melting sweetness". Ralegh was imprisoned for secretly marrying the Queen's Lady-in-Waiting, Bess Throckmorton, and was forced to write his way out of prison. He was banned from Court. He was imprisoned and close to death many times, yet managed to write his way to freedom with a vigour bordering on fury. During his years of disgrace at Sherborne Castle, Dorset, he wrote a striking condemnation of his world, 'The Lie', with such lines as "Say to the court, it glows / And shines like rotten wood, / Say to the church it shows / What's good, and doth no good: / If church and court reply, / Then give them both the lie." [6]

'The Lie' can be read as a defence of "outside thinking" against rigid dogmatism. Ralegh had been accused by Jesuits and pro-Catholics of being an atheist and leader of the 'School of Night', a group that included Dr John Dee, Christopher Marlowe, George Chapman and so on. Although this is a modern name derived from Shakespeare's *Love's Labour's Lost*, in which the King of Navarre says "Black is the badge of hell / The hue of dungeons and the school of night".

Ralegh made his fortune as a man of action centrally involved in the expansion of Elizabethan Protestant England. He established the first English colony in the New World, in present-day North Carolina. He had failures of exploration and lost his fortune. He employed his own magus, Thomas Harriot, as well as having two other mathematician / alchemists / explorers in his household. Harriot was a mathematician imbued in Neoplatonist mysticism. Ralegh had studied with Dr John Dee, royal astrologer, (the inspiration, in part, of Marlowe's *Dr Faustus* and of Prospero in *The Tempest*), and the intellectual leader of Elizabethan expansion and the group of poets surrounding the Earl of Leicester in the 1580s. These included Sir Philip Sidney, Edmund Spenser, Fulke Greville, Edward Dyer among others. They were concerned with rationalising a role for the poet and sovereign within a divine Protestant universe. They saw the poet's role as essentially moral and religious, and sought to renew English as a poetic tongue. English rather than Latin poetry should be used to move English people to virtue and knowledge. Ralegh knew these aristocratic and self-made men well. He was a leading member of what became known as the Sidney-Spenser circle. Ralegh, though, also knew another club of poets, much lower down the social scale: those writers who lived exclusively by the pen. Whereas Leicester's coterie, including Ralegh, lived in mansions along the Strand by the River Thames, these poets and dramatists frequented the margins of London, the theatres to the south of the river at Southwark and to the east in the City of London at Blackfriars and Bishopsgate. Ralegh is credited with being the founder of the Mermaid Tavern's club of poets in 1603. The club included John Donne, Ben Jonson, Christopher Brooke, George Chapman, Francis Beaumont, John Fletcher, Michael Drayton, John Marston, Thomas Dekker and (possibly) William Shakespeare in a floating population of writers, law students and politicians. The Mermaid was a safe house where they could exchange manuscripts and discuss potential patrons and news of court intrigue.[7]

Ralegh is, to me, almost a contemporary. His oeuvre is as fluid as any post-modern critic would want. His name has variant spellings and his words are changed at will. His legendary stories could be claimed as most probable or even fact by a New Historicist critic any day now. In my local weekly paper, the *Blackmore Vale Magazine*, houses are sold with dubious connections to the man. Perhaps his most famous poem, 'The Passionate Man's Pilgrimage' with its "scallop-shell of quiet", "staff of faith" "scrip of joy" and "bottle of salvation" still resonates and is used at commemorative functions.[8]

Ralegh wrote at a time when poets could rapidly run out of favour at court and writing was a dangerous and precarious living. Playwrights and poets that upset courtiers, diplomats, religious leaders and, above all, the monarch, were imprisoned and sentenced to death. You could even be arrested for not writing to order, as happened to Dekker in 1599. Ralegh was tried for treason and atheism several times and won the legal arguments. He wrote much of his poetry in the Bloody Tower where he lived with his family between 1603 and 1616. He only published five poems in his lifetime. His theological, philosophical and poetic work circulated in manuscript form. If the poems got into the wrong hands, it could be well be the end. His accounts of the consequences of tyranny in *The History of the World*, written in the Tower, inspired both John Milton and Oliver Cromwell.

Letter 1: Ralegh

His last poem, 'Even Such Is Time', written the night before he was beheaded, is a pointed survival and partial epitaph, with time paying the narrator nothing but "earth and dust" and its belief that "My God shall raise me up".[9]

Ralegh's head was embalmed and given to his wife. She returned to Dorset, famously carrying his head in a basket, to display that head so that his friends and enemies could say goodbye to him. Bess worked tirelessly to restore his reputation and ensure that his work survived. She kept his head for the next 29 years until her death. Their son, Carew, then took care of his head until his death in 1666 and it was buried with him.

Before I close with my poem inspired, in part, by Ralegh and the transmigration of the soul, I must say that I have come to realise that reading *The Passionate Pilgrim* at age 11, which contained the work of Marlowe, Shakespeare and Ralegh, was an unconscious inspiration for my founding of a theatre company when I was aged eighteen. That company was called The Pilgrimage for Pleasure Theatre and I wrote my first love poems and comedy sketches for that group.

Night Horizons

Looking west to the sounding sea shore
the eternally present in eyes and ears.

Discrete hatching the wood, weed and wag
outside tainted coercion clasped in conjunction.

Light shining in silent stillness before the door
this non person out of action and fear.

Mapping out and mapping subsong of home
racked with flight, darker plumes, pelt in blur.

This prisoner alive with jays and kingfishers
manic to God the sufferer in us all.

Letter 1: Ralegh

Black the night, badge of heat and dungeons
abuses 'stript 'n' spit' into the cauldron.

In this Night School there is no hell eternal,
no damnation, only the soul's ground.

Not born to inherit land or heaven's graces
the substance of things hoped for anchors

This wayward vessel, unearthed to drink
and drink to abandon, disseminate.

Blood drips, coheres into tears and operative
phraseology of sins, transfigured matter

internecine with all forms of lack
and judgment of warring bodies

around the wound from body to text
this scallop shell of quiet unleashed.

Inside the skin creasing compass borne
talisman of shepherds and new worlds

brief ripple of leaves and lineage
earth's shadows fly, black on white.

Beyond those that have power to hurt
this jack, black emissary of dirt, deposits,

stabs and weaves. Twist of hair and moss.
Inside the song. Trail of blood and bit.

Fine hair wisps. Beauty in purpose. Back of throat
longing. Ale and more ale. Head opens to thrill.

Letter 1: Ralegh

Trailed withered root. Multilingual litter brack,
scored with pitch scrapings fed to cattle over-feed

dumped carcass bleeds pink to purple gut
womb intestinal matter left by all but yes

but no but yes but no but butts head feed
pulled water spots wheeling tracks past sings

oh movement continuous untamed and well-
tempted to steal the voice of men.[10]

Notes

[1] William Shakespeare, *The Complete Works*. Oxford: Shakespeare Head Press / Blackwell 1934 p. 244.
[2] Ibid p. 1248.
[3] Florence Emily Hardy, *The Life of Thomas Hardy 1840–1928*. Basingstoke: Macmillan 1962 pp.110–119. Norman Page (ed.), *Oxford Reader's Companion to Hardy* Oxford: OUP 2000, p. 403.
[4] Thomas Hardy, *The Collected Poems*. Ware: Wordsworth Editions 1994, p. 445
[5] The film subsequently appeared as *Elizabeth: The Golden Age*.
[6] Walter Ralegh, *The Poems of Sir Walter Ralegh*, ed. Agnes Latham, London: Routledge Kegan Paul 1962, pp. 45–47. I have followed the modern English rendering as used by Seamus Heaney and Ted Hughes in *The Rattle Bag*, London: Faber & Faber 1982 pp.241–243.
[7] See David Norbrook, *Poetry And Politics in the English Renaissance*. Oxford: OUP 2002, for more details about the Sidney–Spenser group of poets.
[8] Walter Ralegh, *op. cit.* pp.49–51
[9] Ibid p.72
[10] David Caddy, *Man in Black*. London: Penned in the Margins 2007, pp.39–41

Letter 2
Barnes and the English Poetry Canon

I first encountered the poetry of William Barnes when I was sixteen. I had been in Barnes House at Sturminster Newton School and had no real idea of what he wrote until I bought some books at the Dorset Bookshop in Blandford Forum. It was a charming, overflowing bookshop run by two elderly ladies who had published a book about Barnes. What was striking about Barnes was that he wrote almost exclusively in the Dorset dialect. Here was the language that my parents, grandparents, the local farmers, farm workers and villagers, more or less used.

> When skies wer peåle wi' twinklen stars,
> An' whisten air a-risén keen;
> An' birds did leave the icy bars
> To vind, in woods, their mossy screen;[1]

The habitual 'v' for 'f' and 'z' for 's', as in "zunzet" was still in common use. I grew up, as did my daughters, saying, "Oh-arh" and "Look at that girt bull". I come from the same peasant stock as Barnes and at seventeen I was writing a strange poetry inspired by Wordsworth, Barnes and the puns of radio comedy.

I want to talk about Barnes, his context and the English poetry canon. This general overview may cast some light on the narrowness of the canon and the relative instability of late-twentieth-century English poetry.

William Barnes has three aspects that are noteworthy. He wrote for a specific and local audience, the rural poor and dispossessed, and put that focus above anything else. By choosing not to conform to national English he reduced his potential audience considerably. However, his dialect poetry did sell in quantities and has never been out of print. It is still widely available in different editions. Indeed, in the past forty years his position in relation to the canon has improved. There has been a *Selected Poems* in the Penguin Classics series, edited by the then Poet Laureate, Andrew Motion.

Secondly, his work as a linguist and as a theorist of English language is significant and similar to the seventeenth-century Levellers, who also wanted the removal of the Norman-French system of government.

Letter 2: Barnes and the English Poetry Canon

Thirdly, he was also a political economist seeking a way out of worst effects of industrialisation. In other words, there is more to Barnes than might be thought.

The poet, John Ashbery, in a handy book entitled *Other Traditions*,[2] based on his Norton lectures, delineates the value of six poets outside the canon. These include the Northamptonshire peasant poet, John Clare, who is listed in the *Cambridge History of English Poets* among the "Lesser Romantic Poets". He is there with some fascinating figures, such as Barnes, Thomas Love Beddoes and George Darley. Clare is the poet who famously wrote

> I am—yet what I am, no one knows or cares;
>   My friends forsake me like a memory lost:
> I am the self-consumer of my woes—
>   They rise and vanish in oblivion's host
> Like shadow's in love-frenzied stifled throes—
>   And yet I am, and live—like vapours tossed[3]

Now I don't wish to suggest that Barnes is better than Clare. Rather I think that both have been sorely neglected because they deal with the rural poor and dispossessed. Clare lost his mind as a result of his problems and has only recently—thanks to Ashbery, Jonathan Bate[4] and the Clare Society—found his way closer to the canon. A similar resurgence is happening for Barnes. They are, both, though, still outside the canon.

There is a view of the origins of English literary language that late-fourteenth-century and early-fifteenth-century poets took the wrong course within vernacular English as it slowly emerged as a distinct language. At that time the bulk of the population spoke Middle English dialects influenced by successive invaders, the Normans, Vikings, Angles, Saxons and Jutes. The official languages of government were French and Latin and they dominated the Anglo-Saxon and Anglo-Norman dialects. The dialect of London, of the City of London that is, became the first English literary language through borrowings from other languages, the power of print and the position of its users during the fifteenth and sixteenth centuries. The London poets, Chaucer, Gower, Hoccleve and so on, had to make difficult choices about which dialect to write in. It is this borrowing from other languages that so upset Barnes.

One impact of the London poets' choice of literary language is that a cultured English person should know the parts of language that are reliant upon knowledge of Latin, Greek or French and can use them for purposes of power. Similarly the ability to quote from other languages in conversation is seen as the mark of a powerful person. Obviously the less well-educated and poorer people would not ordinarily be able to fully understand such a person.

This affectation towards the quoting of other languages is not confined to the English. Here's Hugh Fox, the American poet, writing about when he first met Charles Bukowski in 1966 and saying

> "You're the first writer I've ever read that used English the way I used it in Chicago when I was growing up. You know, you get a Ph.D., fall in love with T.S. Eliot and Ezra Pound, think that if you write a page without Greek, Sanskrit and Italian in it that you're a fucking fool . . ." [5]

Here is perhaps a key to why Barnes and Bukowski are not acceptable to the English canon, despite tremendous popularity and much academic interest. They use localised versions of English. They write, as it were, in another language. Barnes narrative poem, 'John Bloom in London',[6] for example, when read aloud, comes alive and was a popular part of Barnes' performances. Barnes read his work in and around Dorset and was in regular demand as a popular oral entertainer. He developed a large following and enjoyed a longer performing career than Charles Dickens.

Barnes was a self-educated polymath. Described by Rev. Francis Kilvert in his *Diary* as "half-hermit, half-enchanter", he was far from being an orthodox Victorian churchman. He was more in the visionary tradition of Milton and Blake through his conception of Paradise and out of touch with the direction of Victorian England. He saw Dorset village life as an Other England, an Eden more or less outside of industrialisation. He believed in the holiness of everything and saw God in everything, in all religions. He believed in an everlasting God, without any reliance

Letter 2: Barnes and the English Poetry Canon

upon a totalising theosophy. He was anti-imperialist, spoke out against the Crimean and Opium wars and studied sacred texts in their original language. I went to school with direct descendants of Barnes and Hardy; however, the boy that I most remember is Terry Loveless, a rebellious relative of the leader of the Tolpuddle Martyrs, those farm workers who were arrested for forming a Friendly Society of Agricultural Workers and deported to Australia in 1834. Indeed Hardy can be read as the successful echo of Barnes celebrating a people that live in rhythm with nature and it is the most obvious place to start in seeing the traces of Barnes mark. However, that tradition lived on beyond Hardy.

From the late 1970s until the mid '90s I met various members of the extended Powys family in Mappowder, mid-Dorset. This was the family that produced several writers, poets and artists. John Cowper, of *A Glastonbury Romance* and *Weymouth Sands* fame, Theodore, Llewellyn, Philippa, Lucy and Lucy's son-in-law, Gerard Casey.[7] All were thoroughly intellectual and otherworldly. All were deeply imbued in profound spiritual and literary study. They were not fans of Mrs. Thatcher or President Reagan. They were part of the ongoing inheritance of non-denominational visionary poetry.

Visiting the Powys family was an education. Lucy Powys, youngest sister of John Cowper, and the dedicatee of *A Glastonbury Romance*, had been born in the nineteenth century. Although bedridden, she gave me the second strongest handshake I ever received. A formidable intellect, she chopped at my simple assertions with the discreet charm of an executioner. Taking tea in her summer garden, she was surrounded by butterflies and birds that would congregate around her wheelchair. She was certainly of the same ilk as Blake and Barnes in terms of seeing the living sacrament in all creatures and moment. Barnes, though, was less of a neo-Platonist than she was.

Like Barnes, the Powys family had lived in Dorchester, (Casterbridge in Hardy's novels), a town that in the seventeenth century had been the most godly of Puritan towns.[8] This was a town where power had been exercised according to religious commitment rather than wealth or rank, and there was a tradition of unorthodoxy that Barnes and others fed into. Barnes did not smoke or drink alcohol. Instead he studied philology and the religions of the world. He was a founder and first Secretary of

Letter 2: Barnes and the English Poetry Canon

the Dorset Natural History and Antiquarian Field Club. This society still exists at the Dorset County Museum, Dorchester. His dialect poetry was written for, and concerns the lives of, Dorset agricultural people. Out of the impact of enclosure, the agricultural depression and poverty that so impacted upon John Clare, Barnes developed a middle way between capital and labour in his *Views of Labour and Gold* (1859). His vision of an economy where no one was ever over-worked or idle is a late echo of the seventeenth-century dissenters, the Levellers and Ranters, as well as a precursor to the Arts & Crafts socialism of William Morris. He was a believer in smallholdings, as opposed to the division of labour and the ethos of time-work discipline. The popular image of Barnes in a smock only gives part of the man. Yes, he was anachronistic, an oddball, but he was also a man thinking for the future within a divine universe.

Barnes believed in the local as the starting point of the self and his really big vision, even more than the "small is beautiful" idea, was in the need to restore the English language to its Anglo-Saxon roots. Anglo-Saxon politics were libertarian. You find the Barnes influence in Hardy and the Powys family here. Like Blake, Barnes drew inspiration from ancient Britain with the addition of knowledge of ancient Egypt and Hindu mythology. Barnes was something of an anthropologist and it is no wonder that he was sought out by Tennyson, Browning and other literary figures as a sage. He represented a tradition far removed from the authoritarian Anglo-Norman politics that dominated Victorian England.

Barnes recognised Saxon English as the local language of speech and poetry, carrying with it an alternative culture and civilisation. This is the context of his dialect poetry and the main reason for his exclusion from the canon. He produced glossaries and wrote books on grammar and philology in Saxon English. He had an international reputation as a linguist, having become familiar with some seventy languages. He created a simplified Anglo-Saxon English replacing Latin and French words with new ones. Thus ornithology became "birdlore", pathology, "painlore", optics, "lightlore", and so on. Essentially he used English prefixes and suffixes for foreign ones, thus *many* for "multi", with "multiple" being replaced by *manifold* and "ism" being replaced by "hood", so that equality becomes *evenhood*. He also translated Latin

Letter 2: Barnes and the English Poetry Canon

roots into English so that "-flect" became *bend*, "pose" became *put*, with "preposition" becoming *foreputting* and so on. He also added to Saxon English by creating new words. *Suchness* for "resemblance", *allsome* for "universal", and so on. Some of the words he created and used have been adopted and are now part of the language. *Earthlore* for geology is used by New Age shops and is part of the back-to-nature movement, although, interestingly, it is not in the *Oxford Concise Dictionary*. Also *gawk* from the Dorset dialect, meaning to stand and stare about idly, is well used, albeit recognised as a colloquialism by the *Oxford Concise*. There are many other examples. He made good use of the dialect and there are many words that have been incorporated into the language. It would be interesting to know the full extent of Barnes' success in this. Thanks to Barnes, we can say that the differences between Saxon and Latinate English and the power of each are relatively well known and that for poets word selection, based on knowledge, power and effectiveness, has become an issue that the canon is struggling to recognise and deal with. Barnes' new words have survived but are resolutely kept outside Standard English.

The English poetry canon can be defined as the works and authors represented in the histories and anthologies published by Oxford and Cambridge University Presses. The nature and status of the canon has been challenged since the 1970s on a number of areas, such as the relative absence of women, black, working class and other minorities, and these have been to some extent addressed. However, the position of dialect English, of poets like Barnes, Clare and Samuel Laycock[9], and of the counter-Movement poets of the Sixties, is untenable. Whole traditions are excluded. Essentially, those Sixties poets who absorbed the rich heritage of American poetics from Pound, the Imagists, William Carlos Williams, the Objectivists, the New York School, Black Mountain, San Francisco and the Beats have been ignored and marginalised, despite international success and the publication of a *Collected Poems*. The impact of those diverse poetries was enormous, in stark contrast to the neo-Edwardian Movement poets in terms of developing a counter-culture of poets, poetry magazines and presses in both high and low modernism.

Mainstream English poetry remains conservative, insular and nationalistic. Consider the continued mainstream gloss of Basil

Bunting, with his use and celebration of the Northumbrian dialect, or Sorley MacLean, the Scottish Highlander who wrote in Gaelic, both barely recognised in their own lifetimes. Indeed Oxford University Press (OUP) in New York, but not in Oxford, published by far the most representative anthology of *Twentieth Century British & Irish Poetry*, edited by Keith Tuma in 2001. It was as if Oxford had washed its hands of such brazen openness to The Other. Indeed, J.H. Prynne, one of the most important Sixties poets, refused to allow his work to appear in the volume as an ongoing protest against OUP. Similarly, I have received hate-mail for publishing many American poets and essays on Anglo-American poets and attempting to restore historical accuracy. The OUP and Oxford English faculty have been slow to recognise that the continual refusal to address wider readings of post-1950 English poetry has been a public disgrace and disservice. It goes back to the mid-1970s backlash against the Sixties poets and the rewriting of recent poetic history by such post-Movement poets, and their successors, to suit their own ends. Andrew Motion and Blake Morrison's *Penguin Book of Contemporary British Poetry* (1982) notoriously summarised the Sixties, but excluded the dominant influences on English poetry. Their aim was to establish an alternative to those Sixties poets, with their various art, centred on a few good poets from Belfast. Unbelievable, you might think, but sadly true, and also successful. Their anthology also excluded women and ethnic-minority poets. Motion is now Poet Laureate,[10] and subsequent histories and anthologies have largely excluded what Professor Eric Mottram termed the "British Poetry Revival" until the mid-90s. Such deliberate misreading is slowly being undone.[11]

William Barnes alerts us to the need to study the roots of words and of the need to cultivate local distinctiveness within a wider, international perspective. Like Barnes, I take solace in the knowledge that the English were not always so insular.

Letter 2: Barnes and the English Poetry Canon

Notes

1. 'The Lydlinch Bells' from William Barnes, *Poems of Rural Life in the Dorset Dialect*. London: Kegan Paul, Trench, 1887, p.260.
2. John Ashbery, *Other Traditions*. Cambridge, MA: Harvard University Press, 2001.
3. Harold Bloom & Lionel Trilling, *Romantic Poetry and Prose*. Oxford: OUP 1973, p.578
4. Jonathan Bate, *John Clare: A Biography*. Basingstoke: Picador 2003.
5. Hugh Fox, *Way, Way Off the Road*. Somerville: Ibbetson Street Press, 2006, p.10.
6. William Barnes, op cit. pp.453–456
7. Gerard Casey (1918–2000) was an impressive figure; a poet, translator and thinker. His books include (as Gerardus Cambrensis) *South Wales Echo* (London: Enitharmon Press 1973), *Between the Symplegades* (Enitharmon 1980), *Echoes* (Rigby and Lewis 1990) and *Night Horizons* (Phudd Bottom Press USA 1997).
8. David Underdown, *Fire from Heaven*. London: Harper Collins 1992.
9. See Samuel Laycock, *Selected Poems*, edited and introduced by Glyn Hughes. Sunderland: Ceolfrith Press 1981, for an example of a Yorkshire dialect poet ignored by the dominant culture.
10. Carol Ann Duffy succeeded Andrew Motion as Poet Laureate in May 2009.
11. See e.g. Andrew Duncan, *Origins of the Underground: British Poetry Between Apocryphon And Incident 1933–1979*. Cambridge: Salt Publishing 2008; Robert Sheppard, *The Poetry of Saying; British Poetry and Its Discontents 1950–2000*. Liverpool: Liverpool University Press 2005, and Randall Stephenson, *The Last of England? The Oxford English Literary History Volume 12: 1960–2000*. Oxford: OUP 2004.

Letter 3
Sonia Orwell: The Venus of Euston Road

I first walked along Euston Road, London NW1, in September 1973, on the way to King's Cross St Pancras, one hundred years after Arthur Rimbaud had lived in the area. Here he wrote most of those extraordinary prose poems, *Illuminations*, that transform and allow the reader to see anew. They are filled with bridges, arches and railway lines, as the area is today. It is a fascinating place, layered with literary ghosts. W.B. Yeats lived and wrote at Woburn Walk, from February 1896 to June 1918, and was also involved in an alchemy of the past and future. There is a sense of magnetic attraction to this area that goes back to a time before William Blake's *Jerusalem* (1804–20) mapped a landscape pointing to St Pancras Old Church and the fields north of Euston Road as pivotal.

> The fields from Islington to Marybone
> To Primrose Hill and Saint John's Wood
> Were builded over pillars of gold
> And there Jerusalem's pillars stood[1]

The area and church is named after the Roman boy-martyr executed by Emperor Diocletian in 304 AD. Pancras became a favourite saint in England. Indeed we have a Saxon village here in Dorset named Alton Pancras and its nearby Church Hill. Founded in 314 AD, the Old Church is regarded as one of the oldest in Europe and, with Glastonbury Abbey, the oldest in England. It was built on Caesar's encampment at Pancras called the Brill. This conjecture by the Chief Druid and Antiquarian, Dr. William Stukeley, from his digging in 1750, would have been known to Blake, and was later confirmed by the discovery of Roman bones in 1863 by the Midland Railway Company. This emphasis on field archaeology and the discovery of ancient materials certainly fuelled the late Victorian fascination with the occult and lay behind some of Rimbaud and Yeats' work. Fieldwork has subsequently inspired such poets as Seamus Heaney (*Field Work* 1979) and Peter Riley (*Alstonefield* 2003, *Excavations* 2004) in more diverse ways. According to the *Oxford English Dictionary*, "field-work" is derived from the 'field-work' of 1767, which related to surveying, and that of 1777 when it was first used in connection with agricultural fieldwork. Literary references to "Pangrace" as it was known, include

Letter 3: Sonia Orwell: The Venus of Euston Road

the satirists George Wither, Jonathan Swift, Oliver Goldsmith, where it is cited as a place of great sanctity, and the contemporary satirist, Iain Sinclair, who championed Aidan Andrew Dun's epic poem, *Vale Royal* (1995),[2] on the subject.

In 1865 Thomas Hardy, working as an apprentice architect, supervised the disinterment and removal of coffins to make way for the Midland Railway cutting. These included those of Mary Wollstonecraft and William Godwin, who were removed to lie with their daughter, Mary Shelley, at St Peter's in Bournemouth. During June 1814 Percy Bysshe Shelley had secretly courted Mary Godwin, reading sections of his poem, 'Queen Mab' (1813) by her mother's grave, and her stepsister Jane 'Claire' Claremont. This was the place where Mary had gone since early childhood to escape from her stepmother and where allegedly the boy-poet, Thomas Chatterton, had fallen into an open grave a few days before his death in 1770. Whilst the Old Church was home to radical Dissenters, such as Mary's parents, it was also the place of worship for Catholic émigrés escaping the French Revolution. Church records show a great many members of the extended Blake family using the church but no reference to William, who was involved in the New Jerusalem Church of Swedenborgians elsewhere.

Hardy was imbued by the place,[3] reading 'Queen Mab' and writing several poems about his experiences at St Pancras Old Church, including 'Neutral Tones' and 'The Levelled Churchyard'. The Hardy Tree growing within the old gravestones still exists. The Old Church remains a peaceful place.

In September 1973 I was going to King's Cross St. Pancras to meet a woman. Now, whenever I am in the area, I think of the Venus of Euston Road, and I want to tell some of her story and her literary connections as they impinge upon English poetry.

She was part of a generation of upper middle class bohemian women writers and artists that included Mary Wesley, Lorna Wishart, Barbara Skelton, Caroline Blackwood, Anne Dunn, Joan Wyndham, Elizabeth Smart, Theodora Constantine and Kathleen Raine.

Sonia Brownell was the reluctant muse and eventual lover of members of the Euston Road School of Art and Drawing. From a colonial background, she was educated at the Sacred Heart Convent, Roehampton, the infamous school described by former pupil, Antonia White in *Frost in May* (1933). Sonia's friend and contemporary was the actress, Vivien Leigh. The school left Sonia poorly educated, angry and self-willed. She appeared as a Renoir beauty; insecure, and eager to find her place in a man's world.[4]

Her first affair was with the painter, Adrian Stokes,[5] who became an art critic, linking psychoanalysis and painting, and a poet. Stokes is currently being rediscovered. Both were fascinated by Mallarmé. It is noticeable that Sonia stayed in contact with many former lovers. She was the first networker. She had an affair with Victor Pasmore, one of the founders of the Euston School, and eventually took over his rooms at 18 Percy Street, a short walk from Euston Road. She lived here on and off for the next thirty years. This is next to the Eiffel Tower restaurant where The Poet's Club, of T.E. Hulme and Ezra Pound, met in 1909 and Wyndham Lewis launched *Blast* in July 1914. Sonia also briefly met one of the students, Lucian Freud, who later became a lifelong friend. Freud was another moving onwards and upwards. Her main lover during this time was another founder, William Coldstream, whose wife, Nancy, was having an affair with the poet, Louis MacNeice. Sonia soon knew most of the young painters of Euston Road and beyond.

She frequented the Wheatsheaf pub,[6] close to her Percy Street flat, which between 1936 and 1937 had been one of the main meeting-places of the English Surrealist poets. Rayner Heppenstall, Humphrey Jennings, Dylan Thomas, Roger Roughton and David Gascoyne were all busy translating, discussing and forging ahead within Surrealism. It was, with Zwemmers[7] Bookshop in Charing Cross Road, where the poet and Blake scholar Ruthven Todd worked, a conduit for contemporary French art and poetry. These were the places to go to find out what was happening in Paris and London. At twenty, Sonia soon knew all the players and was part of the social exchange between Paris and London bohemians.

This was an extraordinary time and place for a young woman. Sonia was able to educate herself to an extraordinary level by living here. Poets and painters worked and socialised together in this small area, south

Letter 3: Sonia Orwell: The Venus of Euston Road

of the Euston Road, known as Fitzrovia. It was conveniently close to Bloomsbury, London's poetry publishing centre, and the West End with its theatres, galleries and museums. This was a time when poets and painters were extraordinarily close and Sonia played a significant role in getting people together. She had been won over by the example of Paris and magazines such as *Verve*, (which ran from 1937 to 1960) with contributors such as James Joyce, Ernest Hemingway, Jean-Paul Sartre—originally writing on French cuisine—Pablo Picasso, Henri Matisse etc.

The Second World War did not stop this desire to link art and literature, although Paris was out of bounds. Sonia stayed in Percy Street as the bombs fell. For most young artists it was a time of excitement. As Joan Wyndham, wrote in her wartime diary, *Love Lessons* (1985), "What a life," I said, "never knowing if you're going to be bombed or seduced from one moment to the next!"…

"The bombs are lovely, I think it is thrilling. Nevertheless, as the opposite of death is life, I think I shall get seduced by Rupert tomorrow."[8] And so it was.

Sonia worked at the Ministry of War Transport and helped out at *Horizon* magazine, edited by Peter Watson and Cyril Connolly with the help of unpaid female labour. *Horizon* was, with John Lehmann's *Penguin New Writing* (where Sonia was poached to work for a while), and Tambimuttu's *Poetry London*, one of the leading literary magazines of the Forties. They succeeded Geoffrey Grigson's *New Verse* as the most important poetry magazines and were distinguished by an eclectic mix of art and poetry. Through Watson, Sonia met more painters, including Lucian Freud's friend, Johnny Craxton, Rodrigo Moynihan, Anne Dunn, Graham Sutherland and Francis Bacon, who became life-long friends. Graham Sutherland, for example, would provide the striking cover and illustrations for David Gascoyne's *Poems 1937–1942*, published by Poetry London Editions. Through Connolly, she gained a literary education, and from 1945 became *Horizon*'s driving force as managing editor. Her internationalism and fondness for French and American literature upset many male traditionalists. She read all the submissions, made discoveries—such as Angus Wilson, and argued for her recommendations so well that her voice became the dominant one.

Socially she found herself at the centre of London literary life, hosting parties at *Horizon*, Wheeler's and the Gargoyle Club, with its Matisse-decorated glass ceiling, to celebrate the likes of W.H. Auden, Louis Aragon, Edmund Wilson and T.S. Eliot.

Sonia, through her role at *Horizon*[9] and growing number of contacts, became for a short period immediately after the War a conduit for the entry of French literature into London. She fell in love with her opposite number on *Les temps modernes*, the philosopher, Maurice Merleau-Ponty—a great friend of Jean-Paul Sartre—and with the world of Juliette Greco and Simone de Beauvoir. She befriended a generation of writers and thinkers, including Raymond Queneau, Jacques Lacan, Marguerite Duras, Roland Barthes, Georges Bataille and Michel Leiris. Her mistake with the French, and Merleau-Ponty in particular, was that she did not appreciate the distinction between wife and mistress. She was distraught when the love of her life would not leave his wife for her. She did not understand why he had started and ended the affair, nor where their love had gone.

That generation of French writers and critics, the instigators of existentialism and structuralism, did not really reach England in full translation until the late Sixties or, in some cases, the early Eighties. There was effectively a blockade in the Fifties, through the insularity of the Movement poets and their publishers. *Horizon*, *Penguin New Writing* and the Gray Walls Press, which had fostered an interest in new French and American poetry, closed down and were replaced by editors and publishers who had no interest in internationalism. An interest in modern French and American poetry became very much an underground activity during the early Cold War. Maurice Merleau-Ponty's *Phenomenology of Perception* (1945) was not translated into English until 1962, and only became readily available in 1976. His *Prose of the World*, an intriguing study concerning literary language written in 1952, was not translated until 1973. Merleau-Ponty thus only had a posthumous influence on English poetry, most notably in the work of Denise Riley, John James and J.H. Prynne, where there is testimony that the individual defines the self and the world and is imbued, and or constrained, by conflicting bodies of knowledge. Merleau-Ponty's thinking relates to painting in many ways. It is here that Sonia, with her substantial knowledge of painting since Cézanne, might well have had some impact upon his thinking.

Letter 3: Sonia Orwell: The Venus of Euston Road

Sonia knew all the English writers who contributed to *Horizon, Poetry London* and *Penguin New Writing* and they thought they knew her. She was the acknowledged model for a number of fictional characters, such as the shrewd and efficient Ada in Anthony Powell's *Books Do Furnish a Room* (1967), the bossy Elvira in Angus Wilson's *Anglo-Saxon Attitudes* (1956), the cynical and enigmatic Diana in Marguerite Duras' *Les petits chevaux de Tarquinie* (Little Horses of Tarquinia, 1953) and Julia, "the girl from the Fiction Department" in George Orwell's *Nineteen Eighty-Four* (1949). Orwell's narrator thought that Julia "still expected something from life… would not accept it as a law of nature that the individual is always defeated… All you needed was luck and cunning and boldness. She did not understand that there was no such thing as happiness, that the only victory lay in the far future, long after you were dead."[10]

Orwell saw through her beauty and hard drinking to someone who would fight for the freedom of expression and look after his literary affairs. She had already rejected his proposal of marriage three years earlier. In 1949, on the rebound from Merleau-Ponty, she agreed to marry the ailing man. Three months later, Orwell was dead. Sonia kept his name until her own death in 1980. She looked after the Orwell estate, whilst only drawing a small annual payment from the subsequent massive royalties, and co-editing with Ian Angus the four-volume *Collected Letters, Journalism and Essays* (1968). It was her drive, and methodical tracking down of all Orwell's writing that paved the way for the twenty-volume *Complete Works* (1998), and ensured that Orwell remains one of the twentieth century's dominant literary figures. In many ways this is her lasting achievement. It is in the *Essays* that we find Orwell's best work. In 'Politics and the English Language', first published in *Horizon*, April 1946, 'Shooting an Elephant', 'Reflections on Gandhi' and 'Why I Write' we have some of the most effective English essays written since William Hazlitt. Take, for example, the remark that "Saints must always be adjudged guilty until absolutely proven innocent". The essays continue to be relevant and persuasive to a wide spectrum of thinkers and writers. There is a degree of Anglo-Saxon plain speaking about Orwell that continues to appeal to English readers increasingly despondent with the failure of politicians and with bureaucrats and businessmen who are "economical with the truth".

Letter 3: Sonia Orwell: The Venus of Euston Road

Reading 'Politics and the English Language' reminds us to be continually vigilant against jargon and the sloppy use of English. In recent times, words and phrases such as "political correctness", "celebrity", "cutting edge" and "global village", have lost their meaning through misuse and have become redundant. One of the worst places for jargon has been in English Studies, where some critics manage to swallow a dictionary of jargon that nonetheless enables them to say very little.

Orwell successfully placed a number of new words and phrases, such as "doublethink", "down and out", "Room 101", "Big Brother", "Newspeak" into the English language and Sonia gave us "Orwellian".

Sonia's later years were not particularly spectacular. She worked for the publisher, Weidenfeld & Nicholson, from 1951, overseeing the publication of Saul Bellow, Mary McCarthy and Norman Mailer. Indeed this was a link going back to Orwell, who was the London correspondent of *Partisan Review* magazine. Through this connection Sonia met Bellow, Mary McCarthy, Elizabeth Hardwick, Robert Lowell, Maya Angelou and so on.

Jacques Lacan pursued her in London in an attempt to woo her back to Paris for good. Strangely, Sonia fell in love with Michael Pitt-Rivers, great-grandson of the anthropologist and archaeologist, General Augustus Pitt-Rivers and son of the notorious Captain George Pitt-Rivers, a local fascist who owned most of Dorset,[11] the area where I grew up. Indeed, during my childhood, I heard many stories about this eugenicist and Nazi sympathiser.

Michael was a convicted homosexual and I suppose that a woman who had been hampered in her professional life might be sympathetic to a minority whose activities were against the law. There is also the fact that a great many in Sonia's circle were bisexual. At any rate, it would appear to have been a strategic alliance, giving Sonia financial security and status. It must have been a rare spectacle for the local gentry, farmers and farm workers to be introduced to visiting American poets, French Surrealists, Oxford philosophers and wacky artists in deepest north Dorset. The Captain couldn't hack it and more than once got out his horsewhip to shoo Sonia's guests off his land. When Sonia realised that she had made a big mistake she took a drug overdose, and she divorced Michael in 1961. I can say that, unlike other members of this landowning family, I have never heard a bad word said about Sonia. She seems to have been accepted as "one of those" and that was that.

Sonia returned to editing in Paris producing the magazine, *Art and Literature*,[12] with John Ashbery, Rodrigo Moynihan and Anne Dunn, from 1964–1968. I have the first issue in my hands. It is subtitled 'An International Review' and contains work by David Jones, Gaston Bachelard, Genet, Connolly on 'Fifty Years of Little Magazines', where he acknowledges John Lehmann as the best magazine editor, Adrian Stokes, Kenneth Koch, Tony Towle, the first published poems by David Shapiro, aged 17, and the first publication of an extract from *Wide Sargasso Sea* by Jean Rhys. It is a wonderful mix of English, French and American and, once again, Sonia's selections were successful.

She also translated Duras' plays '*Days In The Trees*' and '*The Square*' for the Royal Shakespeare Company and for subsequent performance in New York. Mostly, she drank and raged against the world. She campaigned to raise funds for impoverished elderly writer friends, such as Jean Rhys and Ivy Compton-Burnett, and wrestled with George Orwell Productions' chief financial adviser to regain control of the royalties and investments that belonged to her and Orwell's son. The money arrived too late. She died of a brain tumour in 1980, penniless in rented accommodation, and Francis Bacon paid for her funeral and cleared her outstanding debts.

Letter 3: Sonia Orwell: The Venus of Euston Road

Notes

[1] William Blake *Complete Writings* ed. Geoffrey Keynes. Oxford: Oxford University Press 1969, 1974 p. 649.
[2] Aidan Andrew Dun, *Vale Royal* Uppingham: Goldmark 1995 p. 94, was inspired by Rimbaud's poem 'Promontoire' as a metaphoric description of King's Cross to research the area in the preparation of his epic poem. The accompanying footnotes are an invaluable guide.
[3] Florence Emily Hardy, *The Life of Thomas Hardy 1840–1928* Basingstoke: Macmillan 1962 pp. 17, 42, 44–45, 131, 189, 277, 304. Reveals the impact of the experience and of Shelley upon Hardy. See also Norman Page, ed., *Oxford Reader's Companion to Hardy* Oxford: OUP 2000 pp. 392–393
[4] Hilary Spurling, *The Girl From The Fiction Department* London: Hamish Hamilton 2002
[5] Adrian Stokes 1902–1972 see http://www.pstokes.demon.co.uk
[6] For more on the Wheatsheaf see David Caddy & Westrow Cooper, *London: City of Words* London: Blue Island 2004 pp. 129–130
[7] For a study of the importance of Zwemmer's see Nigel Vaux Halliday, *More than a bookshop: Zwemmer's and art in the 20th Century* London: Philip Wilson 1991
[8] Joan Wyndham, *Love Lessons* London: Heinemann 1985 p. 112–113
[9] For further information on Sonia's work at *Horizon* see Clive Fisher, *Cyril Connolly: A Nostalgic Life* London: Macmillan 1995; Jeremy Lewis, *Cyril Connolly: A Life* London: Cape 1997; Michael Shelden, *Friends of Promise: Cyril Connolly and the World of Horizon* London: Minerva 1990, and Barbara Skelton, *Tears Before Bedtime* London: Hamish Hamilton 1987.
[10] George Orwell,*Nineteen Eighty-Four,* Introduced and annotated by Bernard Crick. Oxford: Oxford University Press 1984 p. 209, 273. Crick refutes the belief that Julia is modelled upon Sonia, p. 441. Hilary Spurling uses this composite quotation in her biography.
[11] For more information on the Pitt-Rivers see Patrick Wright, *The Village That Died for England: The Strange Story of Tyneham* London: Jonathan Cape 1995 pp.159, 163–171, 177, 260.
[12] *Art & Literature* 1 Eds: John Ashbery, Anne Dunn, Rodrigo Moynihan, Sonia Orwell Paris 1964.

Letter 4: Blake's Marriage

As this is the 250th anniversary of the birth of the poet, painter and engraver, William Blake, and August 12 is the anniversary of his death in 1827, I would like to say a few words about this remarkable figure. At mid-day on Sunday, 12 August, 2007, the Blake Society will be unveiling a new memorial to Blake at Bunhill Fields Cemetery, where he is buried in an unmarked grave. The exact location of his grave is recorded in the Dissenters' graveyard and there will shortly be something more to see at Bunhill.

When I first started visiting London in the early 1970s, William Blake was inextricably linked to the city and the counter-culture that attracted me there.

I had recently bought *Blake: Complete Writings with Variant Readings,* edited by Geoffrey Keynes (Oxford 1969), read Michael Horovitz's poetry anthology, *Children of Albion* (Penguin 1969) and his comments on Blake in *New Departures* magazine, seen Allen Ginsberg on television recalling being visited by the vision of Blake in 1948, and was finding books at Compendium Bookshop, in Camden High Street, such as *The Journal of Albion Moonlight* (1941) by Kenneth Patchen, and *The Kodak Mantra Diaries* by Iain Sinclair, published by Albion Village Press (1971). Blake was linked to the Beats and the hippies as a kind of founding grandfather. At the time this all seemed very special.

However, it was not particularly special at all. Within a year or so I discovered that 1960s' bohemianism was something of a replay of the 1860s, complete with trips to Morocco and India, dropping out and smoking hash, free love, a reverence for and study of ancient religious texts, a fascination with the occult, and so on.

It was in the 1860s that William Blake began to be seen as special, and work began on interpreting his considerable output. Since then, his work has been critically interpreted by successive generations of bohemian writers and artists. From Algernon Swinburne and the Pre-Raphaelites in Chelsea, through John Ruskin, W.B. Yeats, Geoffrey Keynes, Ruthven Todd, Kathleen Raine to Michael Horovitz, E.P. Thompson and Peter Ackroyd.

The first Blake biography was *The Life of William Blake* (1863) by Alexander Gilchrist.[1] Wonderfully vivid and sensational, and based on interviews with many of Blake's surviving friends, it reveals that Blake conversed with spirits, saw angels in trees, sunbathed naked, reciting *Paradise Lost,* with his wife, Catherine, "like Adam and Eve", and greeted his own death with song and faith in the everlasting. This book completely transformed Blake's reputation from being a generally forgotten and ridiculed figure into one of eccentric substance.

Gilchrist, the neighbour of the Carlyle's and Rossetti's in Chelsea, died before the book was complete and it was his wife, Anne, that finished the work, with the help of the Rossetti brothers, and kept it in print. Anne later fell in love with Walt Whitman's *Leaves of Grass,* writing the first critical essay on Whitman and went to live in Philadelphia, with her children, in an attempt to become his wife. They became life long friends.

Dante Gabriel Rossetti had a very bohemian household in Chelsea and amongst his early guests was Algernon Swinburne, an innovative poet and excessive character roughly in the mould of Blake. Swinburne wrote *William Blake: A Critical Essay* (1868), the first substantial critical work on Blake and, like the Rossettis, helped track down Blake's publications. The Pre-Raphaelites clearly saw Blake as a like-minded forebear who was worth celebrating. (Incidentally there is a fine essay on Swinburne by Veronica Forrest-Thomson in the online journal, *Jacket,* issue 20.[2]) Swinburne established the link between Blake and the antinomian tradition and to some extent framed the reference by which we see Blake. By "antinomian" the Victorians mean any religious group that does not obey the moral law of its leaders and does not see such behaviour as necessary for salvation.[3] I prefer to use the term "Dissenter", as it emerged from the seventeenth century because it implies and involves both a political and spiritual dimension, and to see the alchemical and Neo-Platonist traditions as they were transmitted from the sixteenth and seventeenth centuries to the nineteenth as something separate again. This is what I gleaned from my contact with the remnants of the Powys family. Too often, Blake criticism divides into lopsidedness. I think that we need put the social, political and spiritual readings of Blake together. Moreover, we need to recognise that Blake was imbued with the late eighteenth century European alchemical and Neo-Platonist tradition, and to look closely at where his use of language came from. In other words, we need to be historically specific.

Take, for example, the poem 'London' from *The Songs of Experience* (1793),[4] which concerns the mercantile city of London in the 1790s.

It begins with a first-person narrator wandering each charter'd street, indicating with "each" that it is the whole city under review,

Letter 4: Blake's Marriage

and registers the constrictions that he sees on every face. "Mark" and "charter'd" are repeated for emphasis. They embody the stanza's dual sources.

"Mark" and the social "marking" that Blake lists in the poem have a religious framework.[5] The figure of the wanderer in the streets appears in *Lamentations* 4: 13–14 and in *Ezekiel* Ch 9: 4 where we read: "And the LORD said unto him, Go through the midst of the city, through the midst of Jerusalem, and set a mark upon the foreheads of the men that sigh and cry for all the abominations that be done in the midst thereof." Note the use of "sigh" and "cry" from stanza three.

"Charter'd" in the 1790s had a political connotation and refers to the charter that gives rights as well as the charter that established a monopoly and takes away rights. Blake uses "charter'd" in both senses, stressing the loss of rights and implying that they are instruments of injustice. Blake's involvement with the issue of the rights of man began in the late 1780s with his friendship with the St. Paul's Churchyard bookseller and publisher, Joseph Johnson, with whom he socialised, and Mary Wollstonecraft, who wrote *A Vindication of the Rights of Women* (1792), and other radical Dissenters published by Johnson. Blake also knew Tom Paine, who wrote "Every chartered town is an aristocratical monopoly" in *The Rights of Man* (1791). The streets and rivers of London are reduced to the level of sameness by divisive social charters and are marked on the faces of the city. The "charter'd Thames" is a reference to water rights and access to the river for trading and bathing. This is a time when London's rivers are increasingly being used as rubbish dumps. By placing the rights issue within the context of London property, Blake instantly draws in an implicit history of struggle about access, boundaries and divisions between various authorities from the Palace of Westminster (King, Court and Parliament) with the people of the City of London. As a Londoner immersed in City history, he knew about restrictions, the 'every ban' of stanza three.

In stanza two "In every cry in every man" the narrator is himself implicated in the rottenness of society, much as the wanderer in the streets in *Lamentations* is polluted with blood. The stanza reinforces a sense of entrapment by its regular metrical beat and the stubborn insistence of "In". The "mind-forg'd manacles", linking objective manacles of repression and subjective failings, which he sees and hears, are present in his mind as well.

In stanza three the "I" of the opening is replaced by "How" linking the "Chimney sweeper's cry", the horror of which "appals', yet leads to inactivity and thus blackens the Church, "the hapless Soldier's sigh" caught up in a War not of his making, with blood running "down Palace walls". The last line echoing both *Lamentations* 4, with its blind men polluted in blood and, by implication, any recent bloody struggle.

In stanza four the victims from the dark underside of the Church, Crown and marriage speak. Line two's "youthful Harlot's curse", can be read as both her shouting and passing on venereal disease to the infant of line three and on to the marriage hearse of line four, all connected by a cash nexus. Blake ensures that the reader understands that this flow from one to the other is a process by the use of "How" in line two. "How" here also implies that this is a social transaction that is capable of being explored or refused. Mary Wollstonecraft and other radicals saw marriage without love as prostitution and wanted new rights for women.

The poem records the social marking of society, the blackening, daubing with blood, blasts, cursing in the streets and the shocking image of the "Marriage hearse", which can be read as both anti-marriage and the outcome of venereal diseases. Note Blake writes "plagues". The narrator is also marked and aware of the situation with its unavoidable logic that does not depend upon him at all. By the end of the poem these cries, sighs and curses that he hears are tangible signs of shame and active forces of destruction and through the use of the present tense are prophetic, illuminating and terrifying.

Blake made a great impression on the Pre-Raphaelites, including William Morris, and through them, by extension, on the advent of, and visual image of, early Modernist poetry in fine-printed small press publications. The linking figure is W.B. Yeats who, with Swinburne, was the reason for Ezra Pound moving to London in 1908. Yeats was inspired by Blake and William Morris in his desire to be published in handcrafted books, from the Dun Emer and Cuala Presses, using processes outside of mechanical production.

Yeats, published by Elkin Matthews at the Sign of the Bodley Head in the 1890s, was involved in the literary side of the Art Nouveau movement that saw *Dial* (1889–97) magazine, the illustrated quarterly,

Letter 4: Blake's Marriage

The Yellow Book (1894–97) and The Rhymers Club books published. There was a renaissance of artisan hand-based printing linked to creating language for the eye. Pound, Williams, Marianne Moore, Oppen, Laura Riding, and Virginia Woolf's Hogarth Press carried on this tradition.

Poets began thinking more about spatial relations on the page as well as the designs used to frame their work. This work is being carried on today by such presses as Adastra Press in the US and Five Seasons Press in the UK.

Many of Yeats' friends in the Rhymers' Club, that used to meet upstairs at the Cheshire Cheese pub at Wine Office Court, off Fleet Street, were followers of Blake. Poets such as Arthur Symons, John Todhunter and Ernest Dowson met there to drink, smoke hash, and read their work aloud. They were also concerned with cracking the key to Blake's symbolism. None more so than Yeats who, with the artist, Edwin Ellis, produced the three-volume *Works of William Blake: Poetic, Symbolic and Critical* in 1893. Yeats' study of Blake and his circle, Swedenborg, the recently translated Cabbala, and Jacob Boehme, led to the re-discovery of an unknown prophetic book, *Vala, or the Four Zoas*, in the possession of the Linnell family.

Yeats saw that Blake's Four Zoas, or mythological entities, corresponded to the four quarters of London and offered him metaphors and visions, based on alchemy, the elements and zodiac, for an Irish and Celtic revival.

Yeats and Ellis rediscovered other books and their work marked another key stage in the retrieval of Blake's output. Their work was continued and set on a more scholarly footing by Geoffrey Keynes (1887–1982), who first wrote to Yeats in 1913. Keynes was part of the intellectual aristocracy. The elder brother of the economist, John Maynard Keynes, he married Margaret Darwin, a grand daughter of Charles Darwin. Educated at Rugby School and Cambridge, he was a friend of the poet, Rupert Brooke and close to the Neo-Pagans as his brother was close to the Bloomsbury Group. The Neo-Pagans were a loose group of Fabian, back-to-nature bohemians who enjoyed camping and nude bathing.[6] They accepted free love as a principle, but not as a practice. Full of sexual tension, they were dedicated to leisure, art and personal freedom. Keynes became a Consultant Surgeon, specialising in blood transfusion, and spent his spare time on literary scholarship and bibliography. He edited and wrote a dozen books on Blake between 1925 and 1975 and kept on adding to Blake's *Complete Writings*.

The work of Blake's that I currently read most often is *The Marriage of Heaven & Hell* (1790–93). It is a work that I sense will receive more attention in the future. *The Marriage* consists of 'An Argument', 'The Voice of the Devil', 'Memorable Fancies', 'The Proverbs of Hell' and 'A Song of Liberty'. In different editions, plates 4, 14 and 15 are placed in a different order. The distinct sections do not form a sequential narrative. It thus appeals both to a post-modernist and to a historicist sensibility.

Marriage is an alchemical term for the union of male and female, sun and moon, and other opposites. Heaven and Hell immediately invokes Emmanuel Swedenborg's 1778 *Treatise Concerning Heaven and Hell* and Jakob Boehme's *Heaven and Hell* (1622), which repudiates any belief in eternal damnation.

The Marriage is an alchemical text written after Blake's break with the Swedenborgian New Jerusalem Church and for the radical Swedenborgians who were anti-clerical, mystical and Masonic. After April 1789, the New Jerusalem Church began to impose restrictions on its members and no longer accepted sexual love as holy for every member. According to the Church minutes of meetings, there was a fierce battle over sexual rights and privileges, followed by the exclusion of radical Freemasons for supporting the French Revolution. The issues behind *The Marriage* then are rights and liberties.

The Marriage employs inclusive and open meaning within a terminology derived from the seventeenth century mystical and alchemical tradition that was readily available in London bookshops and had been the same sources of dissent for John Milton and the Ranters. (The historian, E.P. Thompson, pioneered this wider approach to the intellectual roots of Blake's mythology in *Witness Against the Beast* (1993). Blake takes from these sources, especially the mystical and metaphysical writings of Jakob Boehme and the alchemical philosophy of Fludd, Agrippa and Paracelsus, and produced his own private symbolism. At root, this satire on Swedenborg is a fusion of theosophy that posits the spiritual tradition, an alchemical union of men and women, against Christian orthodoxy, with its systems of thought from

Letter 4: Blake's Marriage

empirical rationalism based on simple either/or dualisms. It is, in a way, the philosophical primer to the *Songs of Innocence and Experience*. The text works away at attacking certain mental attitudes, "contraries", and is a sustained attack on repression of the divine universe. It shows the reader distinct choices, the "contraries", philosophical and lived dualisms, highlighting passion, the tiger's wrath, excess, exuberance, energy against restraint, doubt, prudence and social control. It delineates two cultures: the untamed devil's and the tamed angelic, a reference to the conservative Swedenborgians, seemingly afraid of sexual liberty. Blake's devil culture vigorously opposes the mental attitudes, the contraries that block sexual freedom, most powerfully expressed in the line "Prisons are built with stones of Law, Brothels with bricks of religion". References to the natural and social world are combined to celebrate human potential and diversity. Blake's distinct contribution to Boehme's theosophy, from which he derives his philosophy of time and eternity, is in the memorable epigrams, such as, "Eternity is in love with the productions of time", "The road of excess leads to the palace of wisdom", "The cut worm forgives the plow" and the child-like allegorical illustrations that are so dissimilar to those in seventeenth century alchemy.

For Boehme, Man is protected by time from sharing the complete suffering of God. He has, though, to share that suffering as the price of entry into eternity. To enter the eternal is to become open to all of the agonies of time and the vision of God, the Alpha & Omega, the eternally present at each time is present in all beings, including animals.[7]

Everything for Blake is not only holy but has a unique nature and perception. The central idea in Boehme's theosophy is that reality in both its physical and metaphysical aspects is a living entity in constant tension between affirmation and suppression of the potential that exists in unity. Contraries, dualisms, yes and no, define each other, bringing forth new forms, new substance within the unity. This is the fundamental philosophy behind *The Marriage*. Blake refuses any neutralisation and easy generalisation of good and evil, heaven and hell, angel and devil, by making the contrasts starker and open to wider meaning. They reside, as the title suggests, in divine man and woman, for whom union is essential. Each epigram, such as "The tygers of wrath are wiser than the horses of instruction", offers a pithy reminder of how to live, and is addressed to all religions, all prohibitions. They attempt to show that individuals, represented by animals as opposed to angels, have different attributes and temperaments that cannot be contained within rules and laws. They create a moral relativism showing that there is no absolute good and evil, citing Milton's interchanging of Christ and the devil as an authority, and placing him with the narrator in the devil's party. Blake's citing of Milton and *Paradise Lost* references for his readers the opposition between the Ten Commandments, a code of prohibitions, and the Gospel of Jesus, a gospel of love and forgiveness, and the seventeenth century political opposition to the Moral Law.

Blake's *Marriage* is an alchemical marriage of heaven and hell requiring the two contraries to remain in opposition, neither submitting to the other, and arises from the energy between both. It is, at once, both a spiritual and political position and Blake proceeds to defend the virtues of desire and energy as marks of liberty.

Since the late Victorian period, Blake has been seen as the exemplary figure of the self-published artisan print-making poet. He acts, as it were, as a reminder of the processed book as commodity and of the ineffectualness of the poetry marketplace. *The Marriage of Heaven and Hell* satirises narrow and dogmatic thinking and offers the diversity of the human and animal world as the site of potential human development. Such a work seems particularly acute and perspicacious at a time of religious conflict, international terrorism and extreme climate change.

Letter 4: Blake's Marriage

Notes

[1] Gilchrist remains a significant source of information. For an account of the earliest essays on Blake see G.E. Bentley, Jr ed., *Blake Records Second Edition* New Haven, CT: Yale University Press 2004 pp. 561–732

[2] Veronica Forrest-Thomson, 'Swinburne as Poet: a reconsideration' *Jacket* 20 at http://jacketmagazine.com/20/vft-swinb.html

[3] For a discussion of antinomianism see E. P. Thompson, *Witness Against the Beast: William Blake and the Moral Law* Cambridge: Cambridge University Press 1993 chapter 2.

[4] William Blake, *Complete Writings with Variant Readings* ed. Geoffrey Keynes Oxford: Oxford University Press 1969 p. 216. See p.170 for the first draft of the poem.

[5] See Heather Glen, 'The Poet in Society: Blake and Wordsworth on London' *Literature & History* 3 March 1976 pp. 2–28 and E.P. Thompson, *Witness Against The Beast* pp.174–194

[6] Paul Delany, *The Neo-Pagans: Friendship and Love in the Rupert Brooke Circle* London: Macmillan 1987; Christopher Hassall, *Rupert Brooke: A Biography* London: Faber & Faber 1964.

[7] Gerard Casey, *Night Horizons* New York: Phudd Bottom Press 1997 pp. 235–241

Letter 5: Ethnopoetics

I first saw the American poet and editor, Jerome Rothenberg, read at the Portsmouth Polytechnic Fine Art Department in 1975. He began by meditating and chanting, and took his audience on a wonderfully disparate journey through his New York and Polish Jewish background to his fieldwork with Native Americans and fascination with archaic and primitive poetries around the world. His willingness to go deeply into his own distinct background and to look beyond at other poetic cultures combined with his sage-like appearance made a deep impression. He seemed to be already a global poet of some distinction. Of course, it was not uncommon in those days for well-known poets to celebrate the works of others in their own readings. I recall seeing Pete Brown, the Liverpool poet, at the Roundhouse in 1974, reciting sound poetry, Scouse poetry, skipping songs, lyrics, street graffiti and expanding the aural expectations of what a poet might do. It was all part of a wider, more open interest in ethnic and non-literate writing, the celebration of diversity and a way of doing things that only poetry can do. Rothenberg and Pete Brown were in their different ways aware of the oral materiality of poetry.

They offer a useful contrast. Brown has subsequently been aloof from the poetry world and forged his own career as an award-winning lyricist, percussionist and band-leader. However, Rothenberg went from translating Paul Celan and Günter Grass in *New Young German Poets* (1959) to the anthologies, *Technicians of the Sacred: A Range of Poetries from Africa, America, Asia, Europe and Oceania* (1968) and *Shaking the Pumpkin: Traditional Poetry of the Indian North Americas* (1972), to becoming the institutional representative of ethnopoetics in America. He has become the epitome of the globetrotting poet-anthropologist-translator-editor, challenging the American poetry canon and helping to extend the history of that poetry.[1] Such a figure as Rothenberg does not really exist in England. Those that sought such a path went overseas rather than face the stubborn refusal to look beyond the island.

Since the Seventies there has been much less openness to diversity in English poetry. Indeed this is something that afflicts both the mainstream and non-mainstream in England. It is more than a Little Englander condition. Just as J.H. Prynne, in his specimen commentary on *Shakespeare's Sonnet 94*, (Cambridge 2001)[2], reminds readers of the etymology and philology of each word in the sonnet, so our

Letter 5: Ethnopoetics

reading patterns have a history that has shaped how we read poems. An awareness of that history, conditioned as it is by ethnic, social, educational, psychological, regional and other factors, and its prejudice, may help us to find the key to those "alien" poems that we refuse. On the macro level, it might help us to appreciate the divide between those who read poems as language only and those who read poems as social process only and show the need to resist closure on either side of the fence.

Beneath that is a deeper condition that refuses both the close reading of each word in every line and the broadest range of possible readings in terms of language effects and imaginative responses and the different levels of meaning of a text and its inter-connectedness within other discourses. Allied to that is the relative lack of understanding within practical criticism that poetry is also a sound. There is an aversion to work that intensifies the materiality of poetry. Thus trite and slick language effects are venerated by the mainstream whilst works with a wider range of effects and meaning are marginalised or excluded.

My poetry reading template was first set in the late 1970s by such books as Raymond Williams' *The Country and The City* (1973), E.P. Thompson's *The Making of the English Working Class* (1968), Jeff Nuttall's *Bomb Culture* (1968), Hugh Kenner's *The Pound Era* (1971) and J.H. Prynne's *The White Stones* (1969). Each book clearly draws the reader into its world and has seminal significance beyond shaping my reading prejudice. As a set it is quite distinct from say, T.S. Eliot's *The Waste Land* (1922), Northrop Frye's *The Anatomy of Criticism* (1957), Robert Graves' *The White Goddess* (1948), Douglas Bush's *Mythology and the Renaissance Tradition of English Poetry* (1963) and Thom Gunn's *The Occasions of Poetry* (1982), a list provided by my friend, Brian Hinton, or a list of post-modernist critics, and is generational. When blanking an alien poem we tend to fall back upon our reading prejudice. Some anti-list and coterie pressure doubtless reinforces that. However, we should try to avoid premature closure of possible reading avenues. Language-based readers should look at social and economic pressures and vice-versa within the context of an understanding that poems are processed as much as a tin of beans.

Letter 5: Ethnopoetics

A decade ago I published some poems by a young woman poet. They were quirky, individual, raw and probing. A few years later she called me to ask why no-one else was publishing her work. She had been rejected. Could I explain what was happening? I fell back on an understanding that mainstream English poetry had become thin and mean-spirited in terms of what it accepts. There is a typical forty-line poem that paints a pretty picture, uses slick techniques, gives a chuckle at the end and amounts to little beyond that. It certainly doesn't lead to any subsequent exploration. That caricature poem and its offspring still prevails and wins all the prizes that are judged by a small coterie of judges, winners and their friends.

I am delighted to say that after some years of rejection Sheila Hamilton has found a publisher in Austria for her first full-length collection. That she had to go to an Austrian publisher rather reinforces my point about the narrowness of English poetry in terms of the primitive and sacred. However, there is more to this. Reading her book *The Corridors of Babel* (Poetry Salzburg 2007)[3], I became aware that her work was more European than English. It is an enlivening work, celebrating psychic, human and natural diversity and the possibility of a wider universe. Hamilton is a "technician of the sacred" to use Jerome Rothenberg's apt term. She is clearly a poet of the earth or more precisely of the universe, that is to say that she is more of an anthropological than an ecological poet. Her brief is thus wider and more concerned with reconnecting and transforming consciousness than mere celebration. She speaks up for a range of abused women through history. Her poems celebrate the range and diversity of birds, fish and animals and their depiction in art, ensuring that the reader becomes aware of their disparate attributes and qualities. They also feature mythological and fabulous creatures such as the unicorn, mermaid, angel, stoorworm, windigo, cath palug, minotaur as they have impinged upon our consciousness and landscape. In sum, her work draws upon the legacy of Claude Lévi-Strauss and the French Surrealists.

The English Surrealist group that came together in the late 1920s and early 1930s blossomed for a short time.[4] They organized the 1936 Surrealist Exhibition at Burlington Place, London. However, they were critically attacked from the outset and only one essay, in F.R. Leavis' *Scrutiny* magazine in December 1932, was sympathetic, seeing the

Letter 5: Ethnopoetics

group as "artisans of a new spiritual progress ... conscious of all the potentialities of human nature". Few survived the Second World War to strengthen and widen their work. Magazines such as *Transition, Experiment, Contemporary Poetry and Prose, New Verse* had closed and new outlets were harder to find. Hugh Sykes Davies withdrew into an academic life. Ruthven Todd and Len Lye went to New York, Humphrey Jennings, Roger Roughton and Dylan Thomas died prematurely and David Gascoyne moved to France. Of these, perhaps only Gascoyne grasped French Surrealism's connection of the spiritual, alchemical and political.

There is no acknowledged tradition of ethnopoetics in English poetry. Sheila Hamilton's fascination with culturally distant forms and lifestyles and her parallel interest in women who are feminist, spiritual, green and Surrealist, such as Remedios Varo, necessarily puts her outside the general reading template of most English poetry editors.

One man who has become synonymous with ethnopoetics did live and work in England for a while and that is Nathaniel Tarn.

Born in 1928 in Paris of British-Lithuanian and French Rumanian parents, he was educated in France, Belgium and England. After graduating in History and English from Cambridge University, Tarn studied Anthropology at the Sorbonne, LSE and University of Chicago, where he completed his Doctorate, based on fieldwork in the Mayan region of Guatemala. He taught at the School of Oriental and African Studies in London. After publishing his poetry volume *Old Savage / Young City* (1964), appearing in *Penguin Modern Poets 7* (1965) and making a celebrated translation of Pablo Neruda's *The Heights of Macchu Picchu* (1966), he became General Editor of Cape Editions and Editor of Cape Goliard Press between 1967 and 1969. Here he published literary, political and anthropological books by the likes of Claude Lévi-Strauss, Roland Barthes, Charles Olson, Louis Zukofsky, Nazim Hikmet, Vaclav Havel, J.H. Prynne and Tom Raworth. I still have many Cape Editions books in my library. This effort to widen the literary horizons of English letters was not entirely successful and in 1970 he moved to the U.S., becoming an American citizen and professor of Comparative Literature at Rutgers University from 1972 until his retirement in 1985. Having battled against Little-Englander resistance to the wider world of poetry, he pursued "Ethnopoetics", the accessing of primitive and archaic poetries. Exiled, and open to other cultures, through extensive fieldwork in Burma, China, Japan, Cuba and Alaska, in a land "full of borrowed" languages, he espouses a universalism. This expansive and enquiring arc from a French to an English and American poet, owes something to the early inspirations of Olson and Lévi-Strauss. Tarn seems to have a genuine psychological and linguistic curiosity about the human mind and condition as well as an abiding sense of where to find deeper layers of history that look backwards and forwards. His non-conformist lineage may be traced from Blake through Yeats, the French Surrealists, Patchen, Dylan Thomas, MacDiarmid to Olson, Robert Duncan and the L=A=N=G=U=A=G=E poets and critics. Being both European and American certainly enriches his perspectives. His latest collection of essays, *The Embattled Lyric: Essays and Conversations in Poetics and Anthropology* (Palo Alto, CA: Stanford University Press 2007), shows the impact of his double career as a poet and an anthropologist and contains some energetic theoretical essays as well as a good amount of biographical information.

Rothenberg and Tarn, both linguists and translators, are fundamentally concerned with finding openings and making connections to the past and future. They have moved out of the Modernist in the spirit of Gertrude Stein's comment: "The exciting thing about all this is that as it is new it is old and as it is old it is new, but now we have come to be in our way which is an entirely different way."

There are translators of Anglo-Saxon and Middle English texts around. Much of this is orthodox and academic rather than creative and anthropological. Again the onus is on closing off the possibilities of sound. The work of Bill Griffiths stands out as an exception to the rule. An Anglo-Saxon scholar, he has an ear for song, the varieties and cadences of speech and writes compacted lyrics that expose layers of social domination. His work is clearly rooted in an oral tradition. His Old English translations include: *Guthlac B* (1986), *The Land Ceremonies Charm, The Nine Herbs Charm* (1986/7), *The Old English Poem 'Phoenix'* (1990), *The Battle of Maldon* (1991). His work is widely published by etruscan books, West House and Anglo-Saxon Books. Will Rowe has recently edited *The Salt Companion to Bill Griffiths* (2007).

Letter 5: Ethnopoetics

There is some anthropologically-influenced work around in England, as Sheila Hamilton's book testifies. Pascale Petit, a Franco-Welsh poet, has had some success with *The Zoo Father* (2001), *The Huntress* (2005) and *The Wounded Deer* (2005), fourteen poems inspired by Frida Kahlo's paintings, and has a strong affinity with natives tribes in Venezuela. Her work is incantatory and works best as a unity.

Dialect poetry has been partially preserved and survives as a mostly backward-looking art. It has perhaps been the Afro-Caribbean poets, now more based in America, such as Kamau Brathwaite, Derek Walcott, that have most effectively taken the art form forward by finding their broader roots. It is notable that many so-called minority poets get absorbed and diluted by the marketing and homogenising process of globalisation.

To find some archaic poetics I would suggest looking at the Notting Hill Carnival procession. The ethos of the costumes, dances and methodology of the participants of this London Afro-Caribbean event is remarkably similar to the Elizabethan and Jacobean Court masques. Indeed it is a fine example of a literary heritage being transported through the Empire and the slave trade to another culture and returning to its country of origin through impoverished immigrants in the 1940s and 1950s. The Carnivals began, I believe, as a response by Afro-Caribbeans in Trinidad to the abolition of slavery in the early nineteenth century.

Claudia Jones, a Trinidadian communist who came to London after being deported from New York as a result of her civil rights campaigning, started the Notting Hill Carnival. Twice interned for her political beliefs on Ellis Island she came to London in 1955. A turbulent character, manic in her energy and astute as a political organiser, she organized the first Carnival in 1959 as a response to attacks on Black people and the race riots of the previous year.

The Carnival which began as a celebration of Caribbean culture and a wider appeal for a united stand against racism, combines the traditional Trinidad Carnival elements of mas, calypso/soca and steel pan with Jamaican-style static sounds, reggae and rap. Non-literate utterances abound and augment and counterpoint the masques of the procession. It is a sophisticated language system at work and a joy to watch.

Notes

[1] There is a useful interview with Rothenberg by Nina Zivancevic in *Jacket* 16 at http://jacketmagazine.com/16/ziva-iv-roth.html
[2] J.H. Prynne *They That Haue Powre To Hurt; A Specimen of a Commentary on Shake-speares Sonnets, 94* Cambridge: privately published, 2001.
[3] Sheila Hamilton *The Corridors of Babel* Salzburg: Poetry Salzburg 2007 See my introduction pp. 7–12.
[4] Michel Remy *Surrealism in Britain* Aldershot: Ashgate 1999.

Letter 6: Salisbury

Travelling on the Damory Bus from my home to Salisbury is an event in itself. The bus company's website and bus-stop timetables offer no reliable information on the service. We rely upon memory that there is a bus leaving the village some time between 9.20 a.m. and 9.40 a.m. and the hope that it continues. So here we are on the bus, filled with retired professionals looking out at the summer landscape. There are plenty of horses and sheep in fields, signs of turf-cutting and wheat ripening. We see deer, pheasant, buzzards and no one in the fields. We pass by Ashmore, with its iconic dewpond, ill-kempt wood and no indigenous population, not far from society photographer Cecil Beaton's old home, Ashcombe House—now occupied by Mr & Mrs Ritchie. The bus falters going up hill as we leave Fontmell Magna and descend deeper into Cranborne Chase, a downland with dense woodland vestiges, Neolithic and Bronze Age earthworks, which straddles parts of Dorset, Hampshire and Wiltshire. The name refers to the land as a place of hunting and has been sparsely populated since Saxon times. It is easy to see the contours of history here. There are houses and entrances designed by the dramatist and architect, John Vanbrugh, and humbler buildings that carry with them the association of bloody struggles between landowners, with their retinue of keepers, foresters and verderers, and poachers. Open an OS map and you will see that struggle in location and place names around the Chase.

Dominated by the Cathedral, with its tall spire and chapter house holding one of the four surviving copies of the Magna Carta, Salisbury is a compact, lively city on the edge of the Plain, a barren chalk plateau to the north west of the Chase. In recent years it has suffered from an overdose of literature development officers and writers-in-residence who visit and leave little behind. This has been happening throughout the country and does not produce local literary communities. In fact, they can be counter-productive. The idea of introducing outsiders as experts, often people at the beginning of their career and without much literary experience, is fatally flawed and a waste of public money. It is a fragmented poetry scene, with people travelling in a thirty-mile radius to attend poetry events, lacking in leadership and direction. There are no magazines or poetry publishers to support the local scene. Yet it has an International Arts Festival and a vast literary history from Sir Philip Sidney, William Browne, George Herbert and Henry Fielding, to Hazlitt, Trollope, Hardy, W.H. Hudson, William Golding and David Gascoyne. John Constable's painting *The Cathedral from the Bishop's Grounds* (1825) is often cited as one of England's best views. It is an extraordinary confluence of place, spirit and identity and is worth investigating in terms of how poets have used the confluence to probe history, identity, and the georgic.

It was in March 1913 that the poet, Edward Thomas, crossed over Harnham Bridge, near the Cathedral, "where the tiled roofs are so mossy, and went up under that bank of sombre-shimmering ivy just to look where the roads branch", on his literary pilgrimage by bicycle from Clapham in London to the Quantock Hills, and Coleridge's home at Nether Stowey.[1] Thomas's journey, with the Other Man, who eats brown bread and monkey-nuts, and whose status is uncertain, has a potent relevance. Although, on the surface, it is a journey searching for signs of spring and observing what is present through earlier poetic responses, it is also a journey of self-discovery, written against the threat of a World War, and a probing of identity, the unconscious, spiritual purpose and landscape looking for rebirth. *In Pursuit of Spring* (1914), is a search for poetic understanding, with Coleridge the dissenter, the "man in black" as Hazlitt called him, as a figurative destination, that is to say, it is a journey which extends from the superficial to the dark and disturbing.

Thomas was moved to have the Other Man quote in full, and with relish, George Herbert's sonnet on sin on his way to St Andrew's Bemerton, where Herbert was rector and died in 1633.[2] It is a chilly, tiny Low Anglican church, with a strong atmosphere of piety, a stained glass portrait of Herbert, and well worth a visit. The adjacent old rectory, rebuilt by Herbert, is now in private hands. My phone call asking to visit was declined.

Thomas cycles on through the Plain, with its five river valleys, interrupted only by a railway line and military camps, noting in this remote and treeless landscape the rooks, pewits and larks. Like Coleridge, Thomas has a fondness for birds (he notes that there are more birds than people in Salisbury that Sunday morning) and is less godly than his alter ego, the Other Man. Just outside Erlestoke he meets two ex-sailors, vagrants, who mention the *Titanic*, bless him and appear to be asking for money, which he refuses to give, and cycles on. He is more concerned with his uneasy conscience than whether the beggars "slept dry and ate enough". Thomas is arguing with himself

Letter 6: Salisbury

about the Christian idea of charity so beloved by Herbert. He is struck by seeing the whole through the inner and outer nature of small things, through the particulars of place, through oppositions, the mildness and wildness of nature, those defining imaginative characteristics he also saw in Coleridge.

Salisbury, its river confluence, the Plain and Stonehenge feature in Song Three of Michael Drayton's *Poly-Olbion, Or A Chorographicall Description of Tracts, Rivers, Mountaines, Forests, and other Parts of this renowned Isle of Great Britaine, With intermixture of the most remarquable Stories, Antiquites, Wonders, Rarityes, Pleasures, and Commodies of the same* (1612), a curious work written in rhyming couplets of twelve syllable lines and engraved maps decorated with goddesses and allegorical figures. Here the traveller-poet uses the marriage and competition between rivers as a unifying symbol. Drayton was part of the Sidney-Spenser literary grouping that came to nearby Wilton House, where Sir Philip Sidney had written most of *The Arcadia* (1590), a prose romance that later so outraged Hazlitt that he called it "one of the greatest monuments of abuse of intellectual power upon record", and *A Defence of Poetry* (1595), which defends poetry as the highest art and equal of nature under God. Mary Herbert, Countess of Pembroke, preserved and published her brother's work after his death in 1586, completed his translation of the *Psalms* and made Wilton into a college of learning, poetry and alchemy. It was the spiritual centre of the Sidney-Spenser movement in English poetry, with many links to poets and writers associated with the Mermaid Tavern in London. Mary was patron to Samuel Daniel, Ben Jonson, Drayton and William Browne. Shakespeare is thought to have attended the 1603 royal performance of *As You Like It* at Wilton. Donne is also said to have visited. Ralegh's half brother, Adrian Gilbert, was her resident advisor and Fulke Greville, as elder statesman of the group, was Mary's most trusted ally.[3]

Drayton's attempt to preserve Albion's history through topography and to forge a national identity was inspired by William Camden's *Britannia* (1586). The "chorography" of the book's title refers to the physical and historical description of a single locality. These included written itineraries and routes across a territory with particular histories, points of interest and local lore.[4] The controlling image of the river stems from Edmund Spenser's 'Prothalamion' (1596). This idea and image fuels *Poly-Olbion*'s celebration of national diversity, with rivers, as loci of conflict and song, serving to unify the country. Drayton essentially produces a map of England based upon rivers and ancient monuments that is linked to ideas of visual memory and national identity. The final part of Book One ends with a celebration of Kentish independence and liberty against Norman yoke and placing Kent as the foremost English shire. William Wordsworth echoes this in 'To the Men of Kent', one of the 'Sonnets dedicated to Liberty', in *Poems* (1807). "Ye, of yore / Did from the Norman win a gallant wreath; / confirm'd the charters that were yours before."[5]

This patriotism is rooted not in Westminster but in the tradition of local defence of liberty. Wordsworth's debt to Drayton is evinced by the many references to rivers and can be read as a kind of up-dated sense of history through topography. Wordsworth as a public poet helped the idea of history through topography further permeate English culture and identity.

Tony Blair's New Labour Government in 1997 somewhat incoherently tried to produce a national brand with its slogan, "Cool Britannia", based on one of Ben & Jerry's ice-creams, using pop musicians as symbols of youthful vibrancy and referring to a transient fashionable London scene. It completely misread how national identity comes to be ingrained as an image and viewpoint as well as the politics behind such images and viewpoints.

The character, Rickie, in E.M. Forster's *The Longest Journey* (1907) sees Salisbury, its converging water, the Plain, its chalk streams, Old Sarum and woods as "the heart of our island". For Rickie as he eulogies on the chalk landscape, "The fibres of England unite in Wiltshire" … "we should erect our national shrine."[6]

In this symbolic and philosophical novel which contrasts the local waterways and "slowly modulating" chalk downs with the quadrangular academic world of Cambridge, Rickie "the lonely and deformed" character recites lines from Percy Shelley's 'Epipsychidion' (1821), at the Rings, that establish the novel's theme and gives it its title. "I was never attached to that great sect / Whose doctrine is that each one should select one mistress or friend and leave the rest 'To cold oblivion' and 'The dreariest and longest journey'." [7]

Letter 6: *Salisbury*

Forster draws upon Shelley's poetry, with its ecological reading, G.E. Moore's *Principia Ethica* (1903), Greek and Wagnerian mythology within a mystical and symbolic structure to delineate his characters difficulties in choosing a life companion. Behind all this, Forster acknowledges an originating experience of talking to a young lame shepherd on Figsbury Rings, whom he offers a tip of sixpence and is declined.

The narrator sees Salisbury as a living creature with powers of movement, and "ugly cataracts of brick" looking "outwards at a pagan entrenchment" and away from the cathedral, neglecting "the poise of the earth, and the sentiments she has decreed". "They are the modern spirit", he observes. He goes on in an unconscious echo of Drayton, although possibly not of Wordsworth. "Streams do divide. Distances do still exist. It is easier to know men in your valley than those who live in the next. It is easier to know men well. The country is not paradise, (an embedded reference to both Sidney's *Arcadia* and Milton) and can show the vices that grieve a good man everywhere. But there is room and leisure."

Forster's sense of national identity is defined, like Wordsworth's, by topography and regionalism, and is in the tradition of Camden and Drayton.

Wordsworth walked across the Salisbury Plain in August 1793, an experience that produced *The Salisbury Plain Poems* (Ithaca, NY: Cornell University Press 1975), 'The Female Vagrant' first published in *Lyrical Ballads* (1798), and fed into *The Prelude*. He changed these poems several times. The unpublished 'Adventures on Salisbury Plain' (1795), a dark gothic poem, concerns a sailor who, having been press-ganged into the navy after war service, becomes a murderer and robber to provide for his family. Penniless and an outlaw, he meets a soldier's widow, as he walks across the Plain. She is homeless, penniless, has lost her family. Both are outcasts and face the inhumanity of Justice. The poem relentlessly shows the human impact of war and links human waste to the historical landscape. This poem was later revised as *Guilt and Sorrow: or Incidents upon Salisbury Plain* (1842) with the image of the sailor's suicide 'hung high in iron case' removed. This self-censoring of the younger, radical Wordsworth is a good example of how the struggles of the rural poor and outcasts can be written out of memory. [8]

Letter 6: Salisbury

J.H. Prynne in *Field-Notes: 'The Solitary Reaper' And Others* (privately published, distributed by Barque Press 2007), points out that W.H. Hudson on his cycle journey through Salisbury Plain (*A Shepherd's Life: Impressions of the South Wiltshire Downs*, 1910 pp 4–5), writes about a young boy, a bird-scarer, running across the ploughed field towards the road merely to see him pass, and consciously neutralises elegiac landscape writing by the avoidance of any polemical, ecological or contemplative input. It is a low-pitch non-poetic narration, without pathos or melancholy, in contrast to Wordsworth's high-pitch narration.[9] Hudson's noncommittal tones and registers, omitting the rawness of the georgic, caught the Edwardian mood of nostalgia for rural ways and were immensely popular. Bird-scaring, though, did not die out in Dorset until the Thirties.

One of this summer's other recommended reads has been Roger Deakin's *Wildwood: A Journey Through Trees*, which will surely join *Waterlog*, his aquatic journey through Britain, as a classic of nature writing in the tradition of Gilbert White and John Stewart Collis. *Wildwood* argues, echoing W.H. Auden, that "the enemies of woods are always the enemies of culture and humanity" and supports this with references from William Cobbett, John Ruskin and various poets. Deakin wanders from place to place seeking out, what Edward Thomas called the "fifth element", wood. He succeeds in his aim "to excite a feeling for the importance of trees through a greater understanding of them" by showing the links between the greenwood spirit and democratic freedom. In particular, he sketches the history of Great Wishford's 1603 charter of rights to collect wood in the Royal Forest of Groveley some six miles outside of Salisbury and the annual May celebration of Oak Apple Day.[10] This requires the whole village "to go in a dance" to Salisbury Cathedral. The villagers legally protected their wood rights at court in 1292, 1318, 1332 and 1825 from landowners eager to use the wood for hunting. The Earl of Pembroke had the manor and wood enclosed in 1809, creating more restrictions, which worsened the impact of the 1820s economic depression. More disputes followed leading in 1892 to the formation of the Oak Apple Club in the village, under the Labour banner "Unity is Strength", to represent wood rights and customs and perpetuate the May celebrations. These involve pagan fertility and other rituals at the parish church and Salisbury Cathedral.

Letter 6: Salisbury

The acorn and oak tree motifs were part of the socialist and anarchist movements defence of liberties. Further disputes occurred in 1931 and 1933 and it was not until 1987 that a new accord was reached allowing the villagers their full rights. The annual Oak Apple Day continues and is an apt reminder of legal victory.

The economic depression following the wars with France, enclosure acts and the Corn Laws, which banned the import of foreign grain and kept the price of bread artificially high, hurt agricultural workers particularly badly as described by William Cobbett's *Rural Rides* (1830) and there were riots in Salisbury. The painter, John Constable was not immune to what was happening and if you compare his *Salisbury Cathedral From The River* (1820), which shows the landscape as a social playground, with *Salisbury Cathedral from the Meadow* (1831), you will see the stark contrast.[11] What is amazing is that the exact spot where Constable painted one of his most literary and symbolic works still exists and when you stand there the painting is more explicable.

Constable portrays two agricultural labourers crossing a stream by horse and cart set against Salisbury Cathedral under a rainbow, after a storm, and next to an outsized ash tree on the left, moving towards a shrivelled ash to the right. In the central foreground is a dog, with a grave to the left and fencing to the right. The ash trees are symbolic of life's disparities, with the Cathedral representing faith and resurrection, and the rainbow hope. The rainbow has to be symbolic as it is in the wrong meteorological place. The dog appears to be observing the scene and directing the viewer's gaze toward the horse and cart, which is empty. They could have delivered grain to the city or come from the city without grain.

Conventionally read, the painting is dominated on the left by the shrub and gigantic ash tree soaring above the distant Cathedral and the illuminated eye of the storm in the mid-central and upper part of the scene. The bright light is at a distance beyond the spire. The shrub and gigantic ash are unadulterated, untamed by reason, a life force, with which the agricultural labourer and waterman are seemingly in harmony. The rainbow encloses the darker half of the painting that is mirrored by the circling stream, representing consciousness and the enduring faith of the labourers in balance with the natural world during an economic and political storm. It is thus an emotional response, with the rainbow of hope encompassing faith and the labourers in harmony with the wildness of the natural world, to the social-political situation. However, when you stand at the exact place that Constable chose and widen the frame of reference you see to the left beyond the Church of St Thomas, is Fisherton Mill where grain was used for bread making and that to the right leads to the older water-mill at Harnham, where grain is used for bread-making and stock feeding. We are thus at the centre of the city's agricultural economy and its supporting relationship to the neighbouring villages. The painting is thus built around an absence of the exact economic conditions that mark the empty cart. The painting has a nine-line quotation from James Thomson's *The Seasons* (1726–30). The *Seasons* was a celebration of the divine order behind the apparent chaos of nature. For the Romantics, including Constable, it was memorable for its descriptions of weather, landscapes, of the moods and colours of the natural world. Mood is dominating economic relations in this painting. Looking again, the dog, separated from the labourers by the stream and on the wrong side to be part of their company, centres the non-economic human connection with the land and acts as a psychological bulwark against wrenching economic conditions.

Constable's cathedral view, often listed as one of England's greatest, serves to show how economic relations, poverty and the struggles behind them are blanked out of cultural memory.

It is a failure to appreciate local history and distinctiveness.

Letter 6: Salisbury

Notes

[1] Edward Thomas, *In Pursuit of Spring* Holt, Wilts Laurel Books 2002 p. 116
[2] Ibid p.120
[3] Adam Nicolson, *Earls of Paradise: England & the Dream of Perfection* London Harper Collins 2008 pp. 99-138; David Norbrook, *Poetry and Politics in the English Renaissance* Oxford Oxford University Press pp. 82–96
[4] William N. West, 'No Endlesse Moniment: Artificial memory and memorial artifact in early modern England' in *Memory Cultures* Eds. Susannah Radstone & Katherine Hodgkin London: Transaction Publishers 2006 pp.61–75
[5] William Wordsworth, *Poetical Works* Eds. E.D. Selincourt & Helen Darbishire Oxford Clarendon Press 1954 p.120
[6] E.M. Forster, *The Longest Journey* London Penguin 1988 p.126
For more on Figsbury Rings see Julian Cope, *The Modern Antiquarian*. London: L Thorsons 1998 p.210
[7] Percy Bysshe Shelley, *Poetical Works* Ed. Thomas Hutchinson Oxford: Oxford University Press 1970 p. 415
[8] William Wordsworth, *The Salisbury Plain Poems* Ed. Stephen Gill Learner Ithaca, NY: Cornell University 1975
[9] J.H. Prynne, *Field-Notes: 'The Solitary Reaper' and Others* Cambridge: privately published, distrib. Barque Press 2007 pp.126–134
[10] Roger Deakin, *Wildwood: A Journey Through Trees* London Hamish Hamilton 2007 pp. 85–94
[11] John Sunderland, *Constable* London: Phaidon 1981 pp. 100–101, 118–109. Ithaca, NY: Cornell University Press, 1975

Letter 7: Bill Griffiths

I would like to say a few words about the poet and translator, Bill Griffiths, who died in September, aged 59, and briefly sketch the context and scope of his work. He produced more than two hundred books and pamphlets and translated from Old English, Welsh, Romany, Latin, Norse and other languages. He was in the tradition of radical pamphleteers, concerned with planting the Liberty Tree, and wrote with commitment to make you think about the words and materials under review. He was concerned with the discourses of power and their effects and with the erosion of local democracy. He had a great ear for music and quickly assimilated speech patterns. Some of his works are beautiful artworks, such as *A History of the Solar System / Fragments: A History of the Solar System* (Writers Forum / Pirate Press 1978). This consists of A4 sheets folded to A5 and machine stitched into a concertina format within green covers. It is a work that literally opens out the world of cosmology, alchemy and belief to show that the universe is multiple and diverse. I have always kept this on my desk to remind me of Bill's inventiveness and that poetry should open out to another place. His passing leaves a large gap in English poetry.

    He was born Brian Bransom Griffiths at Kingsbury, Middlesex, on 20 August 1948. His father was a teacher and his mother had been a civil servant. When I first met him in August 1973 he was known as Billy Griffiths. He arrived at the Windsor Free Festival poetry event, which I had instigated, with his mentor, the sound-poet Bob Cobbing, and read with him prior to another double act, Robert Calvert and Michael Moorcock. He was an impressive reader, using cut-up direct speech and intense syntactical compression in poems about bikers and Vikings. He was like the reading, moody and provocative.

    I met him several times that autumn and kept in regular contact, receiving most of his Pirate Press editions and subscribing to his various books. He was an inquisitive and supportive, albeit argumentative, character. Bearded, with LOVE and HATE tattooed on his fingers, he was part of London's anarchist squatting community and mixed with bikers, Hell's Angels, gypsies, renegade Irishmen and other outsiders. Although he squatted in inner London, writing about the dispossessed in Whitechapel (*Whitechapel: April & May, End, & Start Texts* (Pirate Press 1977), he returned to live at his parental home until he moved into a riverboat at Cowley, near Uxbridge, in the mid 1980s.

Letter 7: Bill Griffiths

He was private and irascible, and I had no idea that he had a degree in Medieval and Modern History from University College, London. He was independent, and radically non-conformist. We argued incessantly about the usefulness of education and how to develop alternative poetic strategies and readerships. I was writing and giving away poems at the time and he urged me to not go to University so that I would think more in alternative ways. This was a time of social and industrial unrest, of fragmentation and protest, and such a proposition was not so fanciful if you had private means, which I did not.

I went to University and this upset Bill, who was committed to the ideals of an alternative society. He made poetry his life, placing it above all other concerns, and was continually producing new work. He employed disparate materials often prefaced by notes based upon his etymological and historical research that alerted his readers to the direction of his thinking. He used juxtaposition and narrative disjunctions to allow other discourses and voices into his poems to add another dimension to the subject under review. Typically, his endings refuse any closure to indicate a situation or event is continuous.

I recall seeing him in spring 1977 when he was strung out and not in great health. He gave a blistering reading at Portsmouth Polytechnic's Fine Art Department. It was a provocative exposure of the mid-Victorian civil service's handling of criminal justice and prisons using found and cut-up texts and documentary evidence. Some of these poems appeared in *Poetry Review* Volume 67 Nos. 1 and 2. He was cleverly using found texts from the past to comment on the present. It was his riposte to my decision to study History and to engage in post-graduate literary study, all part of an argument about theory and practice. His analysis was similar in scope to Michel Foucault's *Discipline and Punishment: The Birth of the Prison* (1977). That night we discussed the Annales School of historiography and the difference in approaches between historians such as the Marxist, George Rudé, and the anarchist, Richard Cobb. The methodological argument between them comes down to the importance attached to the document. Bill's eyes lit up as he extolled the virtues of the document, archives and proper systems of storage and access. Bill later worked as an archivist on several projects, including the cataloguing of Eric Mottram's Archive at King's College, London, and became a member of the Society of Archivists. Bill was, in essence, writing a history of power 'from below', to use the Annales School term.

Bill was an associate of Bob Cobbing's Writers Forum Press and workshop, a regular contributor to Eric Mottram's *Poetry Review*, a stalwart of the Association of Little Presses (ALP), producing the newsletter (PALPI), and Print Shop Manager at the Poetry Society from June 1974. As such, he was an integral part of the London hub—along with such poets as Allen Fisher, Iain Sinclair, Lee Harwood, Gilbert Adair, Ken Edwards and Jeff Nuttall—of what Eric Mottram termed the "British Poetry Renaissance" or "Revival". Bill used the Association of Little Presses bookfairs to sell his hand-printed books and pamphlets and developed his own independent ways of reaching a loyal readership. He produced many publications in the Poetry Society's basement, and several works, including *War w/ Windsor* (Pirate Press 1973), *Idylls of the Dog, King and other Poems* (Pirate Press 1975), *Cycles* (Pirate Press 1975) and *The Song of the Hunnish Victory of Pippin the King* (Earthgrip Press 1976), went into multiple editions. This was a golden age of little-press activity and it was hurting the larger poetry presses. Eric Mottram at *Poetry Review* was accused of publishing too many foreign poets and lost his job. The Poetry Society print shop, where Bill printed his and other London-based publications, was closed down. The whole apparatus of support, including the National Poetry Secretariat, wonderfully administered by Pamela Clunies-Ross, for little-press poets outside London, was taken away. A documentary account of this is given in Peter Barry's *Poetry Wars: British Poetry of the 1970s and the Battle of Earls Court* (Cambridge: Salt Publishing 2006).

His early work includes *War w/ Windsor*, which appeared in several editions, and *Cycles*, distinguished by their disruptive use of language and radical scope. It is in marked contrast to the conventional poetry of that period and takes prison and urban deprivation as its main themes in a sustained study of the manifestations of repression. *War w/ Windsor* explores the social parameters of bikers and the law at a time when the stop-and-search laws frequently used by the police on any individual that appeared to be vaguely outcast. Stop-and-search was based on sections 4 and 6 of the Vagrancy Act (1824) and became a contributory factor in the 1980 St Paul's, Bristol, and 1981 Brixton, riots. Incidentally, his poem, 'The Toxteth Riots' (in *The Mud Fort:*

Letter 7: Bill Griffiths

Selected Poems 1984–2004, Salt 2004) quotes the Liverpool 8 Defence Committee emphasising "police harassment over a long period" as the main cause of the disorder. *War w/ Windsor* gives voice to the biker's world, the Windsor Chapter and Uxbridge Nomads war against each other and the police, of prison and social control, employing broken syntax in linked sets of sound poems that catch their speech patterns in terse narratives. The opening of 'To Johnny Prez Hells Angel Nomads', for example, consists of abbreviated and incremental numbered statements. Thus "1. Christmas straight- / Jacket kid / Packet of light fields / Eye". The vocabulary is severely compressed and honed to a stark aggression. "5. Johnny begot, beading of black Jack-club / Dance kick at drums, can-banging / Death-douce".[1]

    Bill shared the Poetry Sociey's Alice Hunt Bartlett Award for 1974 with Allen Fisher, for such work. Bill augmented his work with his interests in Latin, Anglo-Saxon, Romany, Norse and other languages. The poem 'Cycle 1 (On Dover Borstal)' begins: "Ictus! / as I ain't like ever to be still but / kaleidoscope, / lock and knock my sleeping".[2] "Ictus" being Latin for a physical hit or strike, also signifying the first or regular beat in Latin verse, although there is historical confusion over this (see *Oxford English Dictionary* OED 1), and in medicine the beat of the pulse (OED 2 a), implies impact, stress and a sense of confusion and physicality. The exclamation mark emphasises and raises the pitch of utterance, echoing Romantic exclamatory usage in terms of outcry and suspense. That impact is implied is reinforced by line four's "lock and knock in my sleeping" and that the narrative self is under review is achieved by the switch from the "I" of line two to the "my" of line 4. It continues "the moat (and ported, kinging the blue, closed, so built-made / and the salty grass and rubble of chalk growing / writing the chalk-kid / shout for separation".[3]

    Here the writing shows an educated, disorientated narrator aware of the war machinery at work, "the barbwire is German / it is made with razorblades" and employs alliteration and disjunctions that dazzle and surprise. "You're you / and I ain't any one but you // The bright crazy rings in agate / spring is."[4]

    It is an intensely physical poem, alert to historical knowledge, with a narrator self awake to a landscape and seascape of cuts and bruises and wanting to break free "to think on the pattern of an action". It is this tension of wanting and needing to escape that he dramatically captures.

Letter 7: Bill Griffiths

Bob Cobbing's sound- and visual-poetry workshops at the Poetry Society from 1969–1977 were a formative and continual inspiration. Bill's concern with the materiality of, and ways of scripting, utterances led him back to Old English literature and other languages with traditions of cryptic utterances and runic signs. He also acknowledged in an interview with Will Rowe[5] the impact of Jerome Rothenberg's anthology *Technicians of the Sacred* (1968), with its global ethnopoetics and concern with archaic poetry. The book provided his introduction to works such as *The Nine Herb Charm* (1981), which he would later translate himself.

Bill regularly toured with Cobbing and Paula Claire as Konkrete Canticle, the sound- and visual-poetry group, from 1974 until 1979, from 1984–1988, and again from 1990 until 1992. They toured Canada, Sweden, Germany and the U.K. Here Bill developed different uses for the voice in poetry, fragmenting vowels and consonants, and explored the edges of utterance. As Paula Claire has written in *The Salt Companion to Bill Griffiths* (Cambridge: Salt 2007), Bill continually worked on texts and left behind a whole range of poetic experiments in hypergraphics spanning the repertoire of communication signs in their broadest sense. This is deposited in her Archive.[6]

Through Eric Mottram, who taught English and American Literature at King's College, London, Bill encountered the wide range of poetries published in *Poetry Review* and returned to study Old English at King's, gaining a PhD in 1987. His translation work began with John Porter, working on the late medieval Icelandic texts in *Gisli's Saga – The Verses* (Pirate Press 1974) and then *Beowulf: Anglo-Saxon Text with Modern English Parallel* (Pirate Press 1975). In these and later works, Bill emphasises the rhythmic and would often produce the original text, a literal one and poetic version. His poetic versions though were in marked contrast to standard translations. It was if he was scraping away the Victorian gloss and returning to older traditions through rhythm and sound and placing them in the context of music and dance. His connections at King's College led to a fruitful relationship with Anglo-Saxon Books in Norfolk, who published *The Battle of Maldon* (1991, revised 2000) and *Aspects of Anglo-Saxon Magic* (1996, revised 2003).

In 1990 he moved to Seaham in Durham and became involved in the collection and archiving of dialect materials. His selected poems

Letter 7: Bill Griffiths

1969–1989, introduced by Jeff Nuttall, appeared in *Future Exiles: 3 London Poets* (Paladin 1992). He became Visiting Fellow at the Centre for Northern Studies at Northumbria University. He published *A Dictionary of North East Dialect* (Northumbria University Press 2005), several collections of dialect literature, and wrote some ghost stories set in the baroque world of English local government.

Pitmatic, his last book, concerns North East coalminers and their dialect, and clearly has a socio-political dimension. He remained a political and campaigning poet as is shown by later books, such as *A Book of Spilt Cities* (Buckfastleigh: etruscan books 1999) and *Durham and Other Sequences* (Sheffield: West House Books 2002). Although he also wrote extensively on Plotinus, Darwin and Seaham, it is his consistent writing about struggles between the dispossessed and the police that stand out. See for example such late poems as 'Detective Notes' and 'Thirteen Thoughts as though Woken in Caravan Town at Dawn by 150 Policemen in Riot Gear With Helicopter and Film Back-Up at Saltersgate Near Tow Law in Co. Durham on the Sixth of March 1996' from 1997. Here "communities are moved, / demolition eases the feral-search for ground for housing" and "the opulent win the shadow-box" and "we are subliminated into takens 'n riddle-stanzas / or left a road march". [7]

Bill's poetry has a difficult, edgy surface that is oppositional. It employs an array of languages, often in the same poem or set of poems. Colloquial or spoken English, Anglo-Saxon, local dialects, all collide with Latin, French and Standard English, the written language of power. It his work on the procedures of law and bureaucracy, on prison; his commitment to a locality and its linguistic culture as a base for poetry; his use of ordinary people's lived experience through a musical ear and cut-up disjunctions; his efforts to write polyphonically and to remove the obfuscation of Victorian language over archaic poetries and his continual movement to offset the structures of power with citizenship and the dialect of poetic language that will survive. Bill Griffiths I miss your stubbornness and cussedness already.

Letter 7: Bill Griffiths

Notes

[1] Bill Griffiths, _Collected Earlier Poems (1966–80)_ Hastings: Reality Street Editions 2010 p.119
[2] Ibid p. 64
[3] Ibid p. 64
[4] Ibid p. 65
[5] Will Rowe (ed.), _The Salt Companion to Bill Griffiths_ Cambridge: Salt 2007 pp. 181–182
[6] Paula Claire 'Bill Griffiths: A Severe Case of Hypergraphia' in Will Rowe (ed.) op. cit. pp. 37–50
[7] Clive Bush (ed.), _Worlds of New Measure: An anthology of five contemporary British Poets_ London: Talus Editions 1997 p. 318

Letter 8: In Praise of Walking

Thomas A. Clark, born in Greenock, Scotland, in 1944, writes an attentive poetry, giving space to each word and statement so that it can breathe and linger with the reader. His poetry is also attentive to walking, to the necessity of slow deliberation, and to words and their resonance. I would like to explore walking as a poetic theme using Clark's work as a starting point to weave backwards and forwards.

The first poem in Clark's *Sixteen Sonnets* (Moschatel Press 1981) begins:

> as I walked out early
> into the order of things
> the world was up before me

This neatly situates the narrative self within a prior world of phenomena and perceptions. The "order of things" carrying the phenomena and 'the world was up' denoting the ongoing activity. That phrase "the order of things" is recognisable as the English title of Michel Foucault's study of the epistemology of the human sciences (*Les mots et les choses* 1966, translated as *The Order of Things: An Archaeology of the Human Sciences* 1970) and alerts the reader to questions of the ordering of knowledge and of the interaction between the self and the world. Clark's narrative self walks out into the order of things, that is to say, assuming that things are out there and moving with a sense of attentiveness and becoming. It is therefore a knowing self and walking becomes the act of that knowing self.

The poem continues "as I stepped out bravely / the very camber of the road / turned me to its purpose". The narrator "put design behind' him to 'hear us and deliver us / to the hazard of the road".[1]

Here discovery and the world with all its terrors are already active and the narrative self steps out to build with the hazardous ground as it is. The line "hear us and deliver us" invokes the dissenting tradition of *Piers the Plowman, Pilgrim's Progress,* Milton and Blake and of being delivered from oppression to the promised land. Here explicitly defined as "in all the anonymous places / where the couch grass grows" and enveloped within the echoes of a prayer that is conditioned by temper, with all its variant meanings implied.

For Wordsworth and others walking was seen as an aid to the recovery of memory, creative expression and connecting to the divine. Wordsworth's walking poems, such as 'An Evening Walk', 'The Old Cumberland Beggar, 'The Female Vagrant' and 'Michael' connected walking with poetic labour, poverty and the rural poor. Walking, then, carries within it a subversive content through its associations with poverty, necessity, wandering, awareness and discovery.

From William Hazlitt's 1823 essay 'My First Acquaintance With Poets' we learn that the young Coleridge liked "to compose over uneven ground, or breaking through the straggling branches of a copse-wood; whereas Wordsworth wrote (if he could) walking up and down a straight gravel-walk, or in some spot where the continuity of his verse met with no collateral interruption". [2]

The Romantics set a vogue for walking that was fuelled by guide books and institutionalised by anti-enclosure associations, open spaces and footpath societies and linked to the making of the self. The walking ideology, though, fixes upon walking as an educational experience rather than the cognitive processes of perception, memory, judgement and reasoning that were central to Wordsworth and Hazlitt.[3]

One of my fondest memories of the 1998 Wessex Poetry Festival was Thomas A. Clark's reading early on a Sunday morning, which culminated in a reading of *In Praise of Walking* (1988), a poem consisting of forty statements about walking that weave across the nineteenth century ideology of walking.

In Praise of Walking begins:

> Early one morning, any morning, we can set out, with the least possible baggage, and discover the world.
>
> It is quite possible to refuse all the coercion, violence, property, triviality, to simply walk away.[4]

This deceptively simple poem interjects into an expansive realm of discursive poetics that has been the main path of English poetry and dissent since the nineteenth century.

Clark, in common, with J.H. Prynne, Peter Riley, Geraldine Monk and others, has begun to move beyond the Wordsworthian rupture with the pastoral into new territory.

Following the poem then we note that the world is reached by setting out, again implying ordering, and is there to be discovered, suggesting our knowledge of the world is partial or incomplete and implying an action and a process. The use of "we" suggests that it is possible for us all to discover the world. The "least possible baggage" suggests that closure of thought and emotional response hinders discovery of the world. Discovery, here, implies making connections as we walk and possibly reconnecting with the physical world and human life before or outside of mechanisation.

The second statement acknowledges the possibility of walking away from the world of "coercion, violence, property, triviality". It does not imply withdrawal as such but rather choice. Triviality recalls John Gay's *Trivia, Or The Art of Walking The Streets of London* (1716), an important poem in the history of walking poems. Trivia here refers to the Roman goddess of crossroads, the three ways. This public poem takes the form of a narrated walk through London's streets with a mock classical overlay that advises the reader on the city's perils and the walker on how to dress. There is a lot of waste, sewage and incipient violence. It presents a distorted image of beggars and urban poverty as Tim Hitchcock points out in a new edition of the poem, edited by Clare Brant and Susan E. Whyman.[5] So "triviality" here might signify after Gay an element of frivolity and distortion from the underlying conditions as well as implying a movement away from the unimportant to the important.

The poem's third statement "That something exists outside ourselves and our / preoccupations, so near, so readily available, is our greatest / blessing' registers the connections between the visionary and the primacy of immediate experience. Note the absence of interest in the self and use of the plural in this clear espousal of an undefined world of discovery and visions. Walking is seen as part of the visionary tradition rather than any specific elaboration of a self. This is Wordsworthian then without the self as object. A walk is its own measure.

I am reminded here of John Ashbery's poem 'Just Walking Around' where he writes

> The segments of the trip swing open like an orange.
> There is light in there and mystery and food.[6]

Letter 8: In Praise of Walking

In other words it is the journey that is important and that may involve opening into "light" (vision), "mystery' (the unknown) and "food" (sustenance and thought).

Clark's poem's insistence on the connections between walking and humanness clearly is in contradistinction to those elements of social and economic life where humans are under the constraints of 'time, work and discipline' and of an infrastructure that is eroding those places where it is still possible to walk.

John Barrell in *The Idea of Landscape and the Sense of Place 1730–1840* points out the insularity of local transport systems in that period and travellers' perceptions of the pre-enclosure landscape as mysterious and hostile. Once in a network of paths it was not easy for a traveller to find a way out unless they had local knowledge.[7]

The poem invokes those hidden paths as a reminder of how far the earth has been transformed by transport systems, networks and motorways and how it is still possible to find new ways of doing things.

Kim Taplin has explored the history of footpaths in *The English Path* (Perry Green Press 2000) through the writings of John Clare, William Barnes, Thomas Hardy, Edward Thomas and contemporary poets such as Jeremy Hooker, Ketaki Kushari Dyson, Barry MacSweeney, Iain Sinclair and John Welch. She shows how the network of footpaths connects humans with the natural world as well as place with place and how walking has and still does set boundaries.[8]

Iain Sinclair has developed the London literary walk into a mode of creation, echoing that other London walker, David Gascoyne's *Night Thoughts* (1955), in works such as *Lights Out for the Territory* (1997), where he writes:

"Time on these excursions should be allowed to unravel at its own speed, that's the whole point of the exercise. To shift away from the culture of consumption into a meandering stream."[9]

The poem continues with the powerful line:
There are things we will never see, unless we walk to them.[10]

When I visited the childhood home of the writer, poet and broadcaster, John Arlott (1914–1991),[11] at Basingstoke, I was astounded to find a

Letter 8: In Praise of Walking

tall and pin-thin Gothic building near a cemetery. The cramped living room was seemingly impossible for a family to use. It seemed to be devoid of light. Within and without exuded a distinct aura. There was both a joy and a sadness. This beguiling place began to make sense in relation to Arlott's determination to become a writer, his involvement in the literary world, in the BBC and pubs of Soho, and resonated again with the personal tragedies of his later life. The "Voice of English Summer" indeed had always been surrounded by darkness. In sum, this peculiar house made sense in relation to the life of the poet, cricket commentator and wine connoisseur and I felt that I knew more about Arlott as a result of walking there.

Clark's poem is in argument with or contradistinction to Wordsworth's and other earlier walking poems. The narrator asserts that "What I take with me, what I leave behind, are of / less importance than what I discover along the way". He continues "In the course of a walk we usually find out something about / our companion, and this is true even when we travel alone". Clark's emphasis upon discovery is quite distinct from T.S. Eliot's famous lines from *Little Gidding* (1942): "We shall not cease from exploration" which end with the narrator knowing the place from which they started "for the first time".[12]

For Clark, walking is not so much about knowing as discovering. "A dull walk", he writes, "is not without value". The emphasis is on slowness as opposed to the speed of modern communications and those things we share outside of commercial and monetary value. Making connections, discovery, in this sense concerns reading the landscape encountered. This can take different directions from the materialist to the mystical. From J.H. Prynne through Sinclair to the novelist, John Cowper Powys, who used walking as a way of reaching the elemental and magical world of sensation and transformations.[13] By the way, Jeremy Noel-Tod has written an excellent introduction to the figure of walking in the poetry of J.H. Prynne, in *Necessary Steps: poetry, elegy, walking, spirit* edited by David Kennedy (Exeter: Shearsman Books 2007). There is a sense in which walking serves, in all these writers, as a means of reading, of stimulating connections by motion across the path, the past and present.

The poem asserts that "Wrong turnings, doubling back, pauses and digressions, all / contribute to the dislocation of a persistent self interest". It refuses to give more importance to one meeting or thing above another. For the narrator, walking is egalitarian and democratic. "Walking is not so much romantic as reasonable. / The line of a walk is articulate in itself, a kind of statement."[14]

Here a differentiation is being made between a tourist and a local walker and I take reason to be allied to discovery. It thus implies a movement beyond a Wordsworthian interest in self to a sense of logic as survival. In other words, as a way of discovering how to save the earth from further destruction.

The poem ends by asserting that there is nothing better than to be out walking in clean air and that "To walk for hours on a clear night is the largest experience we can have."[15] The narrator thus reminds the reader that, regardless of difference, we are all part of the universe. This is quite close to Gary Snyder's idea that "walking is the exact balance between spirit and humility." Clark though moves the terrain to the question of value and venerates walking per se as a step towards radical and alternative value. It is, as it were, a movement attendant to the discovery of the world as it is and outside of self interest. Walking connects us with the physical earth and the distant unknown through the motion of moving forwards. It is also a movement from the actual to the possible in cognitive and human terms.

Letter 8: In Praise of Walking

Notes

[1] Thomas A. Clark, 'Sixteen Sonnets' in Clive Bush (ed.) *Worlds of New Measure: an anthology of five contemporary British Poets*. London: Talus Eitions 1997 p.34

[2] William Hazlitt, 'My First Acquaintance with Poets' in *Essays* ed. Charles Whibley London: Gresham Publishing 1913 p.389

[3] Anne D. Wallace, *Walking, Literature, And English Culture: The Origins and Uses of Peripatetic in the Nineteenth Century* Oxford: Oxford University Press 1993 p.166

[4] Thomas A. Clark, 'In Praise Of Walking' in Clive Bush, op. cit.

[5] Tim Hitchcock, 'All besides the rail, rang'd Beggars Lie: *Trivia* and the Public Poverty of Early Eighteenth-Century London' in Clare Brant & Susan E. Whyman (eds.), *Walking the Streets of Eighteenth-Century London: John Gay's Trivia (1716)* Oxford: Oxford University Press 2007 pp.74-89

[6] John Ashbery, *A Wave* New York: Viking 1984

[7] John Barrell, *The Idea of Landscape and the Sense of Place 1730–1840: An Approach to the Poetry of John Clare* Cambridge: Cambridge University Press 1972 pp.87–88, 95–96

[8] Kim Taplin, *The English Path Second Edition* Sudbury: Perry Green Press 2000

[9] Iain Sinclair, *Lights Out for the Territory* London: Granta 1997 p. 7

[10] Thomas A. Clark 'In Praise of Walking' in Clive Bush, op. cit. p.70

[11] John Arlott, *Basingstoke Boy: The Autobiography* London: Willow Books 1990 pp16–17; David Rayvern Allen, *Arlott: The Authorised Biography* London: Harper Collins 1994, has a photograph of the Old Cemetery Lodge.

[12] T.S. Eliot, *Little Gidding* London: Faber & Faber 1942 p.15

[13] Morine Krissdottir, *Descents of Memory: The Life of John Cowper Powys* New York: Duckworth 2007 pp. 49–50

[14] Thomas A. Clark, 'In Praise of Walking' p.71

[15] Ibid p.73

LETTER 9: ALLEN FISHER'S *PLACE*

A great variety of absorbing poetry is obscured by its omission from mainstream publishing, newspaper reviews and the critical narrowness of national poetry awards. There is, at least, a lack of balance dating back to the late 1970s and the changes at the Poetry Society, as described by Peter Barry.[1] National poetry awards are essentially judged by a small coterie of friends who give each other awards, as delineated by *Private Eye* magazine in July 2002, and as Tom Chivers reminded us in *Tears in the Fence* 45.[2] They are essentially unrepresentative of what is and has been happening in English poetry, incredibly safe and unchallenging. There is a tame parochialism and narrowness that has its roots in notions of nation and identity forged between the World Wars and reinforced by the Movement in the Fifties and its apologists in the Eighties. "English decency" as Blake Morrison and Andrew Motion wrote in their introduction to *The Penguin Book of Contemporary British Poetry* (1982). There is an antagonism towards the discovery of meaning and form in language and to reading widely and deeply that flares up in spats about what constitutes poetry and who should control the field. (See for example Don Paterson's 2004 T.S. Eliot Lecture, 'The Dark Art of Poetry', Neil Astley's 2005 StAnza Lecture, 'Bile Guile and Dangerous to Poetry'[3] and their responses. Conversely, there is the predominantly modernist line of thought that seeks to avoid any market taint. (Friends refusing to review friends' work for fear of selling out, for instance.) The "New Generation" Poets of the Nineties and their accompanying marketing machinery similarly adopted a cosy world of vernacular spontaneity and simplistic forms of connection between poetry and life. This strategy involved an acceleration of the critical deterioration heralded by Morrison and Motion. This was not always the case and there are signs that younger readers, thanks to new technology and a greater awareness of other forms of writing, are having no truck with this narrowness.

    I would like to discuss an example of this absorbing poetry that encourages openness and takes the reader off the beaten track and to indicate why there may be signs of change.

I first encountered Allen Fisher's *Place* in literary magazines at Compendium Bookshop in Camden Town, London in the mid 1970s. This was an exciting time to visit Compendium and buy such magazines

Letter 9: Allen Fisher's 'Place'

as *Grosseteste Review, Curtains, The Park, Poetry Information, Aggie Weston's, Joe Dimaggio, Reality Studios, Sixpack, Spectacular Diseases* and Eric Mottram's *Poetry Review*. Scattered amongst such magazines were extracts from *Place* by the poet and painter, Allen Fisher. It seemed like samizdat literature. It was inspirational in the sense that it allowed itself the privilege of drawing upon a wide range of sources that impinged upon South London, where Fisher was born and raised. *Place Book One*, for which Fisher jointly won the Alice Hunt Bartlett Poetry Award, appeared from Aloes Books in 1974 and was followed by other parts of the project, culminating in *Unpolished Mirrors* (Reality Studios 1986) and the complete work finally appeared as one book, *Place* (Reality Street Editions) in 2005.

In common with J.H. Prynne, Andrew Crozier and Iain Sinclair, Fisher drew upon Olson's *The Maximus Poems* (1960), *Maximus Poems IV, V, VI* (1968) and his 'Projective Verse' essay (1950)[4] to articulate a rich seam of sources and information from archaeology, history and geography. I don't think that you can discuss Olson's impact in England without mentioning Ed Dorn's enthusiasm and encouragement to English poets, whilst he was a Fulbright Fellow at Essex University, to follow this path. Raised and educated during the Depression, his poetry was concerned with limits and thresholds of place and identity. Dorn had been taught by Olson at Black Mountain College, lived at Gloucester, the location of the *Maximus Poems,* and clearly was an inspirational figure.

Like *The Maximus Poems*, *Place* is a sprawling work, although not an epic work in the sense of a journey out and in. It is more about process and contemplation than journey. It has a relentless and flat movement forward. The book's organisation is Olsonian, with five main books: *Place Book One, Eros:Father:Pattern, Stane, Becoming* and *Unpolished Mirrors*. *Place Book One* is subtitled in roman numerals I–XXXVII, and contains within it an internal sequence 'Lakes' and a section subtitled 'Making an Essay // Out Of Place'. *Stane*, the Scottish word for stone, is subtitled Place Book III: XLV-LXXXI and so on. There is a complex numbering system at work for each poem or section of the project. There is also a series entitled 'Grampians' that appears in *Place Book One* and *Stane* as well as letters to friends, a response to the publication of Iain Sinclair's *Lud Heat* (1975) and direct quotations from fellow

Letter 9: Allen Fisher's 'Place'

poets, Anthony Barnett and Pierre Joris. There are poems with lines and stanzas at different angles and poems that use horizontal, vertical and diagonal lines to connect bits of text and to allude to other connections. However defamiliarising this might be, it is clearly a development out of Olson, with its shared emphasis on the complexity and plurality of cognition, rather than an imitation. There is no immediately assimilated narrative, *Place* requires the reader to become immersed in the conflicting range of references and readings that constitute its object. The preface states:

> this set takes the form of an essay
> in fragments   that brought together
>   bring about their own symmetry
> their own chaos

and later,

> I await the day when this book will lose & find itself
> in a general movement of ideas. [5]

Place begins by peeling away layers of history and settlement along the Lambeth causeway to the City of London. Through mostly unidentified historical, literary, philosophical and documentary sources, the Lambeth people are shown standing on the sites of battlefields bridging the City banks with cattle fields. Fisher's fragments highlight indices of nineteenth century poverty, submerged pathways and streams, lines of migration and waste, ley lines and boundaries. He seldom attempts to prioritise one fragment over another but rather teases out possible underlying structures and association through juxtaposition. In contrast to the stable identity and formal restraint of Movement and New Generation poets, open field produces polyphonic and fragmented perceptions. On one level there is a kind of levelling of sources and ideas, reminiscent of Eric Mottram's essays, that can engender a less than engaged response. Sometimes the conflicting energies are dissipated, or need to be held in suspension, as other perceptions and lines of enquiry enter the poem. Yet on another, one could argue that Fisher's play on the binaries of the visible and actual, of giving and taking, of sources and deposits,

Letter 9: Allen Fisher's 'Place'

of underlying and artificial divides is an example of an attempted Tao, with its allusiveness intact.

Fisher's achievement in this initially bewildering and subsequently compelling poem is to seek out processes and possibilities and to encourage his readers to embrace this as a work in progress that involves their active participation. In many ways, it was the experience of reading and not understanding *Place* that forced me to make linkages between the concept of place and other discourses that impinge upon any place. In my experience that involved linking with Foucault's discourse analysis and thinking about process and on a practical level realising that a knowledge of place required a full understanding of natural and human sciences as well as social, economic, legal and historical processes. *Place Book One* is entitled *Place* rather than Lambeth or South London and that surely suggests Fisher is attempting to move beyond Williams' *Paterson* and Olson's *Maximus*.

> the loci of a sphere   i have seen it
> I, not Maximus, but a citizen of Lambeth
>   cyclic on linear planes [6]

Here the narrative self, with small and large I to indicate selves, is located in a specific place in the manner of Paterson and the "not Maximus" indicating that this is not an imitation.

This is a long poem with a Shelleyan scope for poetry built upon American models with an English philosophical hinterland. The fifth book, *Unpolished Mirrors*, employs a Blakean flourish with the gardener's, Watling's and Wren's monologues within an enquiry into memory, perception and consciousness that includes references that extend beyond London's literary and scientific history, John Dee and the theatre of memory, to the specialist language of scientific research. Fisher has clearly absorbed Pound, Oppen, Olson, Rukeyser, Reznikoff, Zukofsky and so on. The arrangement of fragments can be seen as both strength and weakness. The strength comes from the emphasis on process, which Fisher develops in later work, such as *Brixton Fractals* (1985), and the weakness comes from the failure to elaborate the interconnectedness of the whole through linkages. I suspect that an underlying resource that Fisher draws upon is A. N. Whitehead's *Process and Reality* (1929), a work that was introduced to me by John Cowper Powys' brother in law, Gerard Casey, in the early Eighties. Although not listed in the bibliographical resources, the work has resonance with the Taoist methodology. Whitehead's central metaphysical idea identifies reality with process. He saw the universe as being in constant flow and change and rejected the dualisms of mind and body, of knowing subject and transcendent object, of man and nature, believing in the interconnection of all things. Another feature is that Fisher includes within the poem some of the background thinking to his work in progress as a kind of estrangement in the Brechtian sense. It can be disconcerting for readers to encounter passages of philosophy with brackets closed and opened. However, this is Blakean in the knowledge that 'without contraries there is no progression' and similarly works to keep *Place* outside of the poetic mainstream and inside a broader avant-garde of poetry as process.

Place's Taoist approach is combined with aspects of late Sixties esoteric research and thinking. These are specifically English sources such as *The Old Straight Track: Its Mounds, Beacons, Moats, Sites and Mark Stones* (1925) by Alfred Watkins and *The View Over Atlantis* (1969) by John Michell, both of which present ley-line theory, and *The Patterns of the Past* (1969), research into underground water systems and ancient sites, by Guy Underwood, a pioneer of earth-energy dowsing. Fisher uses this speculative material on the underlying lines and patterns detected by dowsing to great effect as the Lambeth walker seeking out hidden sources of energy. His contemporary, Iain Sinclair, was similarly divining the past in Hackney, East London, in *Lud Heat* (1975), which along with Andrew Crozier's *The Veil Poem* (1974), is similarly fragmentary and concerned with showing that the world reveals itself, not as a given, but through perception and process.

Place involves much more than I have indicated here.[7] It is the thinking behind a work such as *Place* that is as important as the range and uses made of the content. The poetry may not be as quotable as T.S. Eliot or be as linguistically hinged as Andrew Crozier or as formally elegant as Peter Riley, but it is very effective and works on the reader with repeated readings. Multifaceted long poems such as *Place* are rare and challenging. They are not elitist, per se, as time and scholarship wear them down to manageable tenancies. They are adult and awake, moving forward. There are many ways in and out of their ingenuity. Parts of *Place Book One* echo the connections between the psychogeography of Guy Debord and Raoul Vaneigem and sexuality. There is a sense of fully exploring the relations between the narrator's body and the body of Lambeth. *Place* also contributed to the popularisation of pyschogeography in Britain through its emphasis on walking London and its connection with the large body of work produced by Iain Sinclair. One could also examine the way individual poems mark the extent, through fragmentation, to which the narrative self interjects within certain discourses. *Place* implicitly encourages moral and political thinking, of the need to break out of confined dogmas, peer groups and idioms. It shines as a beacon to show possible ways forward in that endless movement from the natural landscape to the cultural and back again. It makes you consider citizenship, moral responsibility and what it is to live in a place. It makes you think about the limits and thresholds of place, speech, identity and audience.

Time has moved on since *Place* first appeared and we are now a more fragmented and multinational nation, although you would not know this from our national poetry prizewinners. The post-Wordsworthian critique of the pastoral is not merely localised anymore, it is contextualised globally as poetry itself is becoming increasingly contextualised globally. The globe-trotting Australian poet, John Kinsella, has a useful introduction to this in *Disclosed Poetics: Beyond Landscape and Lyricism* (2007).[8] Based in Gambier, Ohio, Kinsella is a remarkable poet of birds and the beach, concerned with issues of nation, place and self that reverberate internationally.

Younger poets and critics are more aware of the twentieth-century English modernist tradition these days thanks to new technological developments. Literary websites, such as John Tranter's *Jacket* magazine, have led the field in essays, articles and new poems within an international modernist aesthetic. Individual poets, such as Ron Silliman[9], have used blogs to discuss a wide range of modernist and other poetries. There are also sites that actively encourage the sharing of wide reading, such as *Goodreads* and *Stumble Upon*, and networking sites, such as *MySpace* and *Facebook*, used by younger people where older poets have made contacts and found a new audience. Younger poets and critics have started their own blogs, such as Edmund Hardy's *Intercapilliary Space*,[10] and display their knowledge and interests. The Internet fosters wide reading through its search engines and, although the information is not always accurate or reliable, there is a great opportunity to discover those marginalised poets of substance that have been almost written out of existence. Combine this with the success of non-mainstream English publishers, such as Shearsman and Salt, and it is broadly possible to say that there may be an underlying change in emphasis under way in English poetry that will eventually see an end to the current ridiculous situation.

Notes

[1] Peter Barry, *Poetry Wars: British Poetry of the 1970s and the Battle of Earls Court* Cambridge: Salt Publishing 2006
[2] Tom Chivers, 'From the Other Side of the Fence' *Tears in the Fence* 45 2006 pp.135–136
[3] Don Paterson's 2004 T.S. Eliot Lecture, 'The Dark Art of Poetry' sourced at www.poetrylibrary.org.uk/news/poetryscene/?id=20 Neil Astley's 2005 StAnza Lecture, 'Bile Guile and Dangerous to Poetry'
[4] Ralph Maud (ed.), *A Charles Olson Reader* Manchester: Carcanet Press 2005
[5] Allen Fisher, *Place* London: Reality Street Editions 2005 p.9
[6] Ibid p.11
[7] Ibid lists sources pp. 409–414
[8] John Kinsella, *Disclosed Poetics: Beyond Landscape and Lyricism* Manchester University Press 2007 pp.1–46
[9] Silliman's Blog is at http://ronsilliman.blogspot.com
[10] *Intercapillary Space* is at http://intercapillaryspace.blogspot.com

Letter 10: Bunting and Fitzrovia

I want to say a few words about the second part of Basil Bunting's poem 'Briggflatts' (1966), which begins:

> Poet appointed dare not decline
> to walk among the bogus, nothing to authenticate
> the mission imposed, despised
> by toadies, confidence men, kept boys,
> shopped and jailed, cleaned out by whores,
> touching acquaintance for food and tobacco.
> Secret, solitary, a spy, he gauges
> lines of a Flemish horse
> hauling beer, the angle, obtuse,
> a slut's blouse draws on her chest,
> counts beat against beat, bus conductor
> against engine against wheels against
> the pedal, Tottenham Court Road, decodes
> […]
> but cannot name the ratio of its curves
> to the half-pint
> left breast of a girl who bared it in Kleinfeldt's.[1]

According to his biographer, Keith Alldritt (*The Poet as a Spy*, 1998), Bunting, a Quaker and conscientious objector from Scotswood-on-Tyne, near Newcastle, may have found refuge in this part of London after having been sentenced to prison in Wormwood Scrubs for 112 days. He had refused to so any agricultural work on the grounds that it would send another man to kill in his place, and absconded from Winchester Civil Prison in June 1919.[2]

Subtitled 'An Autobiography', *Briggflatts* employs a variant sonata form to evoke the shape of a life from childhood to maturity. At the risk of simplification, it has five parts with stated themes moving from innocence with nature and culture in harmony through crisis to resolution. Part one sees youthful love abandoned in the Northumbrian fells in search of a poetic style equal to the mason's craft and wider experience. Part two, mirroring Bunting's own life, sees Fitzrovia, travels to Italy and exile elsewhere. The central part is a Dantesque nightmare concerning Alexander the Great falling off a mountain top at the edge of the world and how peace may be achieved through contemplation and resistance. There is then a move to the Dales and final return to Northumbria with a reflection upon past love and a celebration of skilled labour and other aspects of Northumbrian cultural life. The arc then is from innocence to experience with the Quakerism of part one seen afresh at the end. The poem is imbued with symbolism, Pound's insistence on pruning the inconsequential and a neo-Wordsworthian pastoral. It is also distinguished by a rare sound patterning that is based on the earliest Welsh poetry. The symbolism is not fixed over time. The bull of part one becomes the poet appointed of part two. The riverbed pebbles, slowworm, the beat, and the singing voices of the young lovers recur, slightly changed, throughout the poem and take on new meanings. The symbolism is rather like musical riffs altered by the frame in which it is placed. This use of symbolism is not entirely removed from that of Mary Butts[3] or John Cowper Powys, where function is changed without alerting the reader. And like T.S. Eliot's *The Waste Land* (1922), a key source was Jessie Weston's *From Ritual to Romance* (1920), with its study of the Holy Grail stories and argument that the ultimate object of ritual was initiation into the secret of life, both physical and spiritual.[4]

What interests me in this passage is the gloss over significant experience that leads from a Quaker pacifism to the melting pot of Modernism in London and Paris to involvement in the Second World War and a return to home and the fact that we don't know much about this man and his entry into and departure from Poundian Modernism.

Fitzrovia—bordered by Soho to the south and Bloomsbury to the east, comprises Rathbone Place, Charlotte Street, Fitzroy Street and the surrounding area north of Oxford Street and west of Tottenham Court Road—has come to denote a Bohemian enclave where cultural difference was tolerated between the 1910s and 1950s. The name derives from the fame of the Fitzroy Tavern as a meeting place for writers, artists, musicians, actors, music-hall artistes and outsiders in the 1920s. If you add on its borders you are within the area where the melting pot of Modernist thinking was born in London in the 1910s.[5]

From the nineteenth century Fitzrovia was associated with furniture making and selling; cheap accommodation and entertainment. Successive waves of French, German, Swiss and Italian immigrants, mostly radicals looking for a new beginning, settled there and contributed to the campaigns for the right to vote, to free education and for women's rights. They also opened shops and restaurants, specialising

Letter 10: Bunting and Fitzrovia

in their own cuisine, adding to the large number of coffee houses and inns in the area. The proximity of art schools in Bloomsbury meant that this was an attractive place for artists, art students and artist's models. The immigrant-led business community quickly realised that they could cultivate the bohemian avant-garde and that both would prosper.[6]

The Austrian chef, Rudolf Stulik, made the Eiffel Tower Restaurant fashionable by encouraging Wyndham Lewis, Nancy Cunard and their literary friends to become regulars. It was here in 1909 that T.E. Hulme's Poet's Club—including the subsequent founders of Imagism, F.S. Flint and Ezra Pound—met, and where Wyndham Lewis launched the Vorticist magazine, *Blast*, in 1914. In March 1919 the naturalised Polish Jew, Judah Kleinfeld. who had made greatcoats for the army, converted the German Tavern, The Hundred Marks, into the Fitzroy Tavern and cultivated musicians and artists. These and other proprietors helped nurture and cultivate a climate of religious, political, class, and racial and sexual difference. Aristocratic bohemians intermingled with dancers from the Windmill Theatre and petty criminals on the streets of Fitzrovia. This social and cultural mix was particularly conducive to literary and artistic endeavour as a bolt-hole where they could be anonymous. The Wheatsheaf pub near the Fitzroy became the meeting-place for Surrealists in London in the 1930s.[7] It is quite clear that Bunting is drawing attention to the role of this place in his life and in Modernist poetics.

The lines "Poet appointed dare not decline / to walk among the bogus, nothing to authenticate" might indicate that a higher authority has assigned the narrator the post of poet within a group or society and that this appointment "to walk among the bogus" is on a level playing field of authenticity, suggesting that all are equally inauthentic or as authentic as one another. For a Quaker authenticity is at the heart of holiness and so the "nothing to authenticate" might indicate that the poet-narrator is no longer a believer, holy or equally unholy. Holiness for a Quaker involves humility, self-giving, and a movement towards self-knowledge. Thus, the "mission imposed" is not merely the mission to find a suitable poetics, it is also one to achieve self-knowledge. The passage end indicates that the narrator uses sex to get from one person to another and is sickened by the self-maiming. All of this leads to a "still-born" poetry.

Given that Fitzrovia would become a playground for displaced intellectuals and spies, such as Anthony Blunt, Guy Burgess and Donald Mcclean, and that Bunting worked in Intelligence in Iran, the reference to "Secret, solitary, a spy" certainly implies the narrator as observer as well as active agent. Indeed Bunting would eventually receive patronage; become "a kept boy" and go to jail in Paris, an experience that galvanised the writing of 'Villon' (1925), and doubtless be "cleaned out by whores". The description of these lines though, more generally, evokes the bohemian life of a struggling Twenties Fitzrovian poet. An inhabitant of a floating population of tricksters, con men, salesmen, would be artists and writers. I am reminded of the artist, Nina Hamnett—the former lover of Modigliani and Anthony Powell—after the Second World War, "touching up acquaintance for food and tobacco" at the Fitzroy Tavern. An object of pity adored by Dylan Thomas and ridiculed by Francis Bacon, she perhaps has become synonymous with Fitzrovia's downside and mated "beauty with squalor".

Re-reading the passage in comparison to others, it uses a rational language of measuring and calculation, "he gauges / lines", "the angle, obtuse", "counts beat against beat", "the ratio of its curves / to the half-pint" and so on that leads to a description of alienation, self-disgust and artistic sterility. Note the use of "lines" as in poetic line and "counts beats" as in musical time, a recurring theme within the poem. This may indicate that the passage concerns Modernism as a poetics of exile and urban rootlessness reflected by juxtaposition and alienation. The subsequent stanzas echo this concern with 'calculation' and 'elucidation' indicating that a measuring of the poetic line and poetic course is being questioned.

The "half-pint / left breast of a girl who bared it in Kleinfeldt's" is a reference to Nina Hamnett, who allegedly gave Bunting a copy of Ezra Pound's 'Homage to Sextus Propertius' (1919).[8] This poem impressed Bunting with its use and variety of rhythm more than its critique of empire. It was the movement away from Victorian sentimentality and rigid poetic line that caught Bunting's senses. Whilst the passage is clearly pointing to Fitzrovia and to the narrator's experiences, unlike Alldritt, who provides little supporting evidence, I have been unable

Letter 10: Bunting and Fitzrovia

to find compelling evidence to place Bunting at Kleinfeld's before October 1925. Indeed one of the problems is that Kleinfeld's does not really become a regular bohemian meeting-place until 1926, when Nina Hamnett and her circle decided that it would be a place to meet away from the tourists that were observing them at the Eiffel Tower Restaurant, Café Royal and elsewhere.

Hamnett's circle included the composers Philip Heseltine (Peter Warlock) and Cecil Gray, the writers, Mary Butts, Jack Lindsay, Wyndham Lewis, the poets Tommy Earp and Roy Campbell, the artists, Augustus John, Jacob Epstein, Christopher Nevinson, and their various friends and lovers. Hamnett was also connected to the Socialist group that met in Charlotte Street, through artists, Jacob Kramer, William Roberts and the *New Coterie* magazine, edited by the anarchist, Charles Lahr, between November 1925 and 1927, which published D.H. Lawrence, T.F. Powys, Robert McAlmon, Hugh MacDiarmid, Liam O'Flaherty, H.E. Bates and Nancy Cunard. It was a circle that was imbued in Symbolism as much as Vorticism and clearly tolerant of a divergent Modernism.

From 1926 the composers, Constant Lambert, who lived in nearby Percy Street, and E.J. Moeran, Hamnett's lover from Spring 1927, used to play their compositions on Kleinfeld's electric pianola. Philip Heseltine, founding editor of *The Sackbut*, a music journal, who shared a love of bawdy limericks with Hamnett, was often to be found at a table with two or three young women. Cecil Gray, Michael Birkbeck, and other composers also went to Kleinfeld's to enjoy the liberal atmosphere and make connections. Bunting's extensive knowledge of early and contemporary music would certainly not be out of place within this environment. Kleinfeld allowed his customers to behave as they wished, tolerating unconventional dress and homosexuals of both sexes. Sketches by artists and short scores by composers that fill Kleinfeld's daughter, Annie's autograph book enable us to date their presence with some certainty.[9] Bunting's presence at this time coincides with his writing for *The Outlook* magazine in 1927 and his becoming music critic in October 1927. This is after the writing of 'Villon' and gives rise to serious doubts about Alldritt's and other accepted versions of the chronology of events, relations and influences.

Letter 10: Bunting and Fitzrovia

The "left breast of a girl that bared it in Kleinfeld's" is close to the description given by Hamnett when Dylan Thomas introduced Ruthven Todd to her in 1935, "You know me, m'dear—I'm in the V & A with me left tit knocked off!"[10] This was a reference to Henri Gaudier-Brzeska's statue *Torso of Nina*; Gaudier, the French Vorticist sculptor and Hamnett's former lover, was killed in the First World War, and was the subject of a biography (*Gaudier-Brzeska: A Memoir*, 1916) by Ezra Pound. Bunting is thus making several references in one line. Hamnett's two memoirs[11] reveal a fondness for name-dropping aristocratic bohemians and parties, as well as not revealing identities and of obscuring events by hiding people—a Fitzrovian tradition continued by John Arlott, Daniel Farson and others in their memoirs. There is no mention of Bunting. Indeed Bunting is absent from all of the Fitzrovian memoirs and biographies that I have read. Hamnett, though, reveals a bohemia that veers from erotic encounters to anonymous identities wanting to live outside the law. Bohemianism is a state of mind that is outside of the usual time, work and discipline ethos. Idleness, pleasure-seeking, creativity and living precariously without conventional employment are the norm. Neither Bunting nor Hamnett had the independent wealth of a Nancy Cunard, Mary Butts or Philip Heseltine and there's the rub. Hamnett failed to find new outlets for her art and eventually spent more time drinking and talking about her Parisian past than creating. Hamnett's gradual fall into alcoholism began at Kleinfeld's when she resorted to drawing visitors for money and eventually drinks. In the end, she would do anything for money.

The fact that Bunting's early life in London and Paris is essentially still unknown and that we still do not have an edition of his letters hinders our understanding of his subsequent life and his poetry. Hamnett or Mary Butts may have introduced him to the world of the erotic during the post-War revelries. *Briggflatts* is an eroticised poem, infused with desire, through the pebbles and slowworm and use of verbs which echo that play. It is also suspicious of the sublime or transcendental, of the kind of occult concerns that fascinated Heseltine and Butts when Bunting probably met them at Kleinfeld's. However, it is close to Butts in its "magic of naming". Butts—the great-granddaughter of

Letter 10: Bunting and Fitzrovia

William Blake's patron, Thomas Butts—had attended Pound's Soho gatherings (which had replaced the ones originally started by T.E. Hulme) and was married for a short time to the poet and publisher, John Rodker. She was featured in Louis Zukofsky's *An Objectivists' Anthology* (1932) with Bunting.[12] Rodker, also a conscientious objector who had been imprisoned during the War, published Pound's *Hugh Selwyn Mauberley* (1919), *The Fourth Canto* (1919), as well as Eliot and the Vorticists, replaced Pound as foreign editor of *The Little Review* and worked with James Joyce in Paris. He was someone whom Bunting might have met in the early twenties in London and, through him, met Pound. Moreover, his poetry, like 'Briggflatts', employs no masks, no self-censoring or ironic distancing. Butts' novels, *Ashe of Rings* (1925) and *Armed with Madness* (1928), combine stream-of-consciousness with a complex symbolism. She had similar magical and mythological preoccupations to those of Yeats and John Cowper Powys and was championed by Pound long after her death in 1937.[13] Butts and Rodker offer a different methodology to Pound and a challenge to the kind of Modernism that he represented and to which 'Brigglatts' is knowingly moving away from. Butts left Rodker for a succession of affairs, a short-lived obsession with Aleister Crowley and the occult, and developed a neo-pagan spirituality. Butts was also part of Ford Madox Ford's circle in Paris, a close friend of Stella Bowen, and visited Pound in Rapallo in 1923. There are plenty of unknown relationships and untouched correspondences to give rise to the thought that this passage holds more than on the first few readings. How, for example, do we respond to "Buddha's basalt cheek" and who "shopped" the narrator? Bunting is certainly drawing attention to this place and these people and his role as a poet in that bohemian environment. The key concept to me is authenticity, involving, for a Quaker, the movement towards self-knowledge, and that in 'Briggflatts' is to be found in the Northumbrian localism and its vocabulary that the poem espouses.

Letter 10: Bunting and Fitzrovia

Notes

[1] Basil Bunting, *Collected Poems* Oxford: Oxford University Press 1978 p.43
[2] Keith Alldritt, *The Poet as Spy: The Life and Wild Times of Basil Bunting* London: Aurum Press, 1998. pp.23–30
[3] Mary Butts, *Ashe of Rings and Other Writings* New York: McPherson & Company, 1998.
[4] Morine Krissdottir, *Descents Of Memory: The Life of John Cowper Powys* New York: Duckworth, 2007. p.253
[5] Peter Brooker, *Bohemia in London: The Social Scene of Early Modernism* Basingstoke: Palgrave Macmillan, 2004.
[6] Mike Pentelow & Marsha Rowe, *Characters of Fitzrovia* London: Chatto & Windus, 2001. pp.1–33; David Caddy & Westrow Cooper, *London: City of Words* London: Blue Island, 2004 p.121.
[7] Caddy & Cooper, op. cit., pp.129–130
[8] Alldritt, op. cit., p.27
[9] Sally Fiber, *The Fitzroy: The Autobiography of a London Tavern* Lewes: Temple House Books, 1995. pp.15–26
[10] Ruthven Todd, *Fitzrovia and the Road to York Minster* London : Michael Parkin, 1973. p.5.
[11] Nina Hamnett, *Laughing Torso* London: Virago, 1932, 1982 and *Is She A Lady?* London: Allen Wingate, 1955.
[12] Nathalie Blondel, *Mary Butts: Scenes from the Life* New York: McPherson & Company, 1998. pp.33–68
[13] Ibid pp. 96–150

Letter 11: Tom Raworth's Comedy

I first encountered the poetry of Tom Raworth in Michael Horovitz's *Children of Albion: Poetry of the 'Underground' in Britain* anthology (Penguin 1969) and *Penguin Modern Poets 19* (1971) when I was at school. I was struck not only by the various art of the poetry but also by its comic touch. It immediately signalled a playful inventiveness that has since been developed over more than forty years.

Raworth was born in south-east London in 1938. He became a mature student at the University of Essex's Literature Department in 1967. Prior to this, he had a variety of clerical jobs and taught himself to set type and print. Between 1959 and 1964 he produced *Outburst* magazine and books under the Matrix press imprint. From 1965 he ran the Goliard Press, with Barry Hall, until Jonathan Cape Limited bought it in 1967. He published work by Edward Dorn, Anselm Hollo, Elaine Feinstein, Ron Padgett, Tom Clark, Charles Olson, Robert Creeley and his own first book of poems, *The Relation Ship* (1966), which won the Alice Hunt Bartlett Prize in 1969. He also printed books by Louis Zukofsky, Ted Hughes, Dom Moraes and Basil Bunting for other presses. He was thus at the centre of the Renaissance in English Poetry in the sixties.

At Essex, under the aegis of Donald Davie, Raworth consolidated friendships with Dorn, John Barrell, Ted Berrigan, Creeley and Olson. All of these connections are evident in his *Collected Poems*[1] through a rich intertexuality of naming and dedication. After being Poet-in-Residence at Essex in 1970, he began giving regular reading tours in North America. From 1972 he lived in the US, until he returned to England in 1977 to be Resident Poet at King's College, Cambridge, the city in which he continued to live until very recently. Since then he has made his living from writing books, residencies, and reading tours in Europe, Africa and North America. He belongs to that tradition of English poets who are essentially and necessarily internationalist. His graphic work has been shown in France and Italy, and he has collaborated and performed with musicians, painters and other poets around the world. In 1991 he became the first European writer to be invited to teach at the University of Cape Town for thirty years.

Raworth's early work has a philosophical and comedic eye that produces poignant two-liners such as:

> i cannot prove a second ago
> to my own satisfaction   (*Collected Poems* p. 105)

> trust marginal thoughts
> some like shoes will fit   (*Collected Poems* p. 51)

> puff! i've put it out with my hand
> and you all understand   (*Collected Poems* p.108)

Avoiding the Movement's parochialism, Raworth explores within, rather than through, language. The early poems often compress a number of discourses into a succinct form, marked by the use of fragmented short lines and a multiplicity of word play within free verse forms. The social certainties of post-war Britain lose focus and slide rapidly into a newer, fresher world in this poetry.

I want to take a look at the possible sources for Raworth's comedy: the sudden juxtapositions, comments, asides and disrupted narratives that are infused with comic twists and turns that are a hallmark of his poetry. The connections between Raworth, the New York School, Black Mountain and Pop Art have been examined elsewhere.[2] However, in his 1972 interview with Barry Alpert, Raworth tends to underline his independence from such influences, knowing of course that those movements were built on older ones and that the non-literary can impinge upon poetry as much as the discursive. By taking a different angle we may contribute to a wider contextualisation of his early work. In *Act* (1973), a title redolent of meaning and yet self-consciously mocking at the same time, the act of re-writing is signalled from the start in the first section, 'Nine Poems' where 'nine' is crossed out and 'mine' hand written above the typeface. Other interruptions follow and the reader is forced to think differently through omission, unexpected juxtapositions and an unpredictable playfulness.

Raworth's early work from 1963 to 1980 was surely informed by the gradual liberalisation of post-War Britain, the creation of the welfare state, imperial decline and the erosion of the ideals of the optimistic sixties counter-culture. As a child he would have had memories of the Second World War and post-war shortages and austerity. As a teenager he would have been part of the first generation of youngsters to have surplus income for pleasurable pursuits. He would have heard the Tory Prime Minister, Harold Macmillan, say in 1959 that "most of our people have never had it so good" when the growth of consumer capitalism

Letter 11: Tom Raworth's Comedy

was underway. He would also have experienced the tremendous growth in new technology during that and the subsequent period. These events saturate the frames of his poetry. He would know the echoes of "winds / of change" that "shift / if that's / what reality is" (*Collected Poems* p. 220). Raworth would have also listened to the radio as a teenager and surely would have encountered Spike Milligan's *The Goon Show* (1951–60).

The writing procedures employed by Milligan in *The Goons* and the *Q5* television series, which contributed new words to the vernacular and so inspired the creators of *Monty Python's Flying Circus* (1969–74), were a development out of BBC radio comedy dating back to *It's That Man Again* (*ITMA*), 1939–49, written by Ted Kavanagh.

Ted Kavanagh's *ITMA* played with the sound and meaning of words, employed puns, alliteration and bursts of comic rhyme within unusual narratives. Thus from *ITMA* No. 28 Fourth Series April 1942:

CECIL	Will there be swings and things?
CLAUDE	There'll be coconut shies I surmise.
HANDLEY	Yes, and merry-go-rounds, you hounds.
CECIL	There'll be side-shows, Mose—

ITMA began the trend of quick-witted humour in radio comedy with its sudden twists.

CECIL	Then we'll have a dekko Sir Echo.
CLAUDE	We'll have a penn'orth Sir Kenneth.
HANDLEY	Yes, you'll get a shock Sir Cock – now away you go.[3]

ITMA mercilessly attacked officialdom and officiousness, the Office of Twerps, and the opposing axis powers through the absurdly sinister and creepy-voiced Funf character. It was a trend that was continued by Kenneth Horne and Richard Murdoch's *Much Binding in the Marsh* (1944–54), which subverted and stretched the conventions of radio comedy in what started as a complaint against Royal Air Force (RAF) bureaucracy, the word "binding" being RAF slang for complaining. Like, Kavanagh, they were habitués of the Fitzroy Tavern and the BBC pub, the George Inn, at 55 Great Portland Place, where they mixed with other actors, poets, radio producers, musicians and composers. After the

Letter 11: Tom Raworth's Comedy

Second World War, these pubs and those in between in Fitzrovia and Soho were not only places to socialise but also to find work and develop new literary and comedic ideas. For example, the main instigator and creative force behind Kenneth Horne's *Beyond Our Ken* (1958–64) and *Round the Horne* (1965–68), Marty Feldman, lived in Soho Square in 1949, and was encouraged to write poetry and comedy by Dylan Thomas.[4] Ted Kavanagh and Thomas were also associates and planned to write film scripts together in spring 1951.[5] Feldman followed the bohemian path to Paris where he became immersed in existentialism. He returned to Soho intent on becoming a scriptwriter. Like Milligan, he would later read poems in his television comedy programmes as another layer of absurdist self-revelation. Milligan also presented *Muses with Milligan*, a poetry-and-jazz television series, in 1964. Feldman and Milligan famously worked together on the award-winning *Marty Feldman Comedy Machine* in 1971, where the visual comedy in sketches such as the Auto Mechanic, the Bomb Squad and Undertaker are clearly existentialist. The absurdist and existential writing of self-educated bohemians such as Milligan and Feldman should be distinguished from the early Sixties boom in satire that was largely written by Oxbridge-educated public school boys inspired by *The Goons*. Incidentally, J.H. Prynne features Kenneth Horne in his poem 'Viva Ken'.[6]

Written by Spike Milligan against the backdrop of the atom bomb, the Cold War and a post-War Britain of shortages and Imperial illusions, *The Goons* subverted the language of authority, bureaucracy and the military with funny voices, broken and interrupted narratives and a private vocabulary of new words, army slang, grunts, squeals, giggles and a wide range of bizarre sound effects. It was a comedy that employed sound poetry and absurdist humour in quick-fire avalanches of associated word play. This can be read as a comedic equivalent to poetic enjambment and juxtaposition. It is widely read as surrealistic as the scripts are multi-layered, where each line is an event, often involving more than one intention and meaning and conventional narrative is subverted by elision, the intrusion of extraneous concerns and sidetracks which become dominant.

Both Raworth's poetry and *The Goons* employ fast, free form word play.

Letter 11: Tom Raworth's Comedy

> Read Me
> thanks   (*Collected Poems* p.138)
>
> Marley is dead.
> No, I'm not.
> BANG
> Yes you are.[7]
>   (*Goon Show A Christmas Carol* 24 December 1959)

It is not just the speed that is similar but it is also the freedom of association and disassociation that enables Raworth and Milligan to explore beyond or disrupt any simple narrative. Both are quickly distracted and move on to the next thing. There is more than a possibility that different voices may be present in each line. They wander off in and around absurdity and use quick-fire humour to mask an anger and disgust at what they observe. The comedy has its roots in protest. They are both surely pushing the bounds of their art form.

In the *Goon Show Call of the West,* 20 January 1959, the script purports to be a television western on "your radio screen" where the sound effects call for "the whole audience [to] scream and run for the exits". The first narrator, unable to read more than "The Pling-plang toof noppity nippity noo, plita. Omnivirous, plethora. Platty plong plong to te to ti tue ... fnit, poll. Tong, tang ting, putt putt ..." stops and says "I say, I can't read this rubbish I ... Ooo!", and is killed off. His falling in the water receives the riposte from Seagoon, "Yes sonny, it's a tradition among drowning men", who takes up the narrative. Milligan uses Seagoon in the next line to attack the myth of America as the "land of plenty" and has him hit a bum. The con man Grytpype-Thynne and his downtrodden sidekick Moriarty, who is also heading west and wants to be let of a "retired wooden fish-crate", join him in the next line.[8]

Raworth's *Act* (1973) contains poems that could have been written by Milligan's character, Eccles. Raworth and Milligan's comedy of disjunction and fast flowing word association are joyful explorations from the constraints of a coherent self. Both excel at blurring the boundaries between one voice and another, one narrative and another, and cut across their own work with drawings and asides as if their work were boundless.

Letter 11: Tom Raworth's Comedy

    Surgical Names: John
    every home has a sharp knife
    where's the sharp knife?   you had it in the garden
                                     (*Collected Poems* p.93)
    Surgical Names: Frank
    heads
    tails   (*Collected Poems* p.95)

    Taxonomy
    the albatross drawer
    this is the drawer where we keep the albatrosses
                                                 (*Collected Poems* p.97)

Each line and sound in *The Goons* is an event that forces the action forward and outwards to an extreme of language use or an irreverent joke, or both.

    Here's some more from *Call of the West* 20 January 1959:

GRAMS:	NIGHT. DISTANT CRICKETS. DISTANT HOWL OF A PRAIRIE DOG
SEAGOON	I say, will those prairie dogs never stop howling?
GRYTPYPE-THYNNE	They're always howling, no trees on the prairie.
SEAGOON	Listeners who recognise that gag please keep their traps shut … Well, I'm going to bed … Goodnight.
GRAMS:	GREAT SQUEAKING AND COMPRESSING OF BED SPRINGS. BREAKING, CREAKING, ETC
SEAGOON	Eighteen-stone, gad I'm a heavy sleeper.[9]

Raworth is in essence the poetic equivalent of Spike Milligan. Both are easily distracted with continual tangents off any perceived narrative. In both cases rhythms weave in and through a series of narrative selves that are primarily mechanisms of forward movement. This is particularly

Letter 11: Tom Raworth's Comedy

evident in Raworth's long thin poems, most notably *Ace* (1974) and *Writing* (1982). The poems are a natural development from earlier work, such as *Act* (1973) and *The Mask* (1976). Here, as in Olson's dictum that "One perception must immediately and directly lead to a further perception", the poems incorporate a wider range of perceptions, from overheard conversations, bits of autobiography, references to new technology and scientific equipment, pop lyrics to more discursive materials and are more fragmentary.

My experience of listening to *Ace* and *Writing* and other poems read at Birkbeck College, London, in May 2003, was not unlike listening to *The Goons*. The poems are read in performance as quickly as the eye falls upon the word. Members of the audience laughed at odd times as the sudden jokes and quirky word play of the narratives filtered through. I recall Will Rowe, the presenter, mentioning the half-time break and Raworth joking, "You can have a break whenever you want" and members of the audience following the reading with copies of the *Collected Poems* losing their way and sitting back with wide grins. It was a joyous and celebratory occasion. Raworth is adept, like Milligan in his use of gags, at placing a deft two-liner when the reader / listener may be lagging behind the speedy narrative.

> put your money
> where your eyes are   (*Collected Poems* p. 264)

> 'have you a headache?'
> 'no I'm looking
> out of my right eye'   (*Collected Poems* p. 301)

Both Raworth and Milligan ultimately register the primacy of the act of writing and employ similar fragmentary approaches involving forms of erasure, omission, unexpected layering and movements off and unprecedented levels of energy.

Notes

[1] Tom Raworth, Collected Poems. Manchester: Carcanet Press 2003
[2] See for example Peter Robinson, 'Tom Raworth and the Pop Art Explosion' in *Twentieth Century Poetry: Selves and Situations*. Oxford: Oxford University Press 2005 pp. 206-229
[3] Ted Kavanagh, *The ITMA Years*. London: Woburn Press 1974 p. 51
[4] See interview with Marty Feldman *The Montreal Gazette* 7 August, 1977 p.33 sourced through Google
[5] Paul Ferris, *Dylan Thomas: The Biography*. London: J.M. Dent pp. 270–271
[6] J.H. Prynne, *Poems* Tarset: Bloodaxe Books, 2005 p.154
[7] Spike Milligan, *The Goon Show Series 10 Episode One* sourced at http://www.thegoonshow.net/scripts_show.asp?title=s10e01_a_christmas_carol
[8] Spike Milligan, *More Goon Show Scripts* London: Woburn Press 1973 p. 76
[9] Ibid pp.77–78

Letter 12: Poetry and Celebrity

I thought that I might approach the idea of celebrity and issues around that cultural phenomenon in relation to English poetry.

Initially I thought of Barry MacSweeney's brush with celebrity in 1968, when his publisher, Hutchinson, nominated him for the Oxford Professorship of Poetry at the age of nineteen, following the success of his first book, *The Boy from The Green Cabaret Tells of His Mother* (1968), and of how he turned away from the marketing plans of a large publisher to embrace the small and independent presses and a more profound approach to poetry. MacSweeney maintained a sharp eye on public events and language culminating in his unpublished 'Mary Bell Sonnets'. The fact that these remain unpublished put a scupper on sketching how celebrity impacted upon his work.

Secondly, I thought of John Clare's direct experience of the impact of Lord Byron's celebrity as he watched Byron's funeral cortège of sixty-four carriages travel through London in July 1824, and of Clare's own short-lived time as an object of curiosity as a rural poet,[1] and how he mangled his own identity with that of Byron's celebrity in those extraordinary poems written when he was hospitalised in Epping Forest. In July 1841, having been at High Beach Asylum for three and a half years, Clare's explorations of identity and experience culminated in his mixing of Byron's identity and birthday with his own. He had been constantly shifting from his versions of *Don Juan* to *Childe Harold*, from Bryon's model of sexual freedom to his own sexual losses, and finally united his inner and outer worlds by walking out of the hospital and back to his home in rural Northampton. Once the conflation of Byron's identity and freedom with his own situation and that of the rural poor is complete, he musters the necessary will to attempt to break free.

However, in that journey he unravels the workings of the marketing of a poet. He begins his version of *Don Juan*: "Poets are born and so are whores", echoing Byron aurally by punning on "cant" and "cunt" in the second line, and condemns himself as a poet-whore restricted by his own material conditions. For Clare, poets are not born but formed by economic circumstances and the market place. "So reader", he writes, "now the money till unlock it / & buy the book & help to fill my pocket."[2] The poem continues employing a sound and meaning nexus around the words "canto", "cant", "cannot", "can't", "cunt", "cunning" and "coney" and attacks the vanity and display of poetic fashion.

Byron was arguably the first modern celebrity. He played, to quote Marilyn Butler, "a larger part than any other single artist in shaping the stereotype soon recognised throughout Europe, the passionate, rebellious Romantic Poet."[3] Greece declared a day of national mourning upon his death. News of his gallant death spread across the major towns and cities of Europe. The cult of Byron impacted upon artists, composers, musicians and writers throughout Europe reaching Russia and Scotland. Many people who had never known him were saddened by the loss. The fourteen-year-old Alfred Tennyson never forgot the day when he heard the news, remembering it as "a day when the whole world darkened for me".[4]

John Clare noted the impact of Byron's death upon ordinary people in contrast to the scoffing at his fame.

> "… the Reverend the Moral and fastidious may say what they please about Lord Byrons fame and damn it as they please—he has gained the path of its eternity without them and lives above the blight of their mildewing censures to do him damage—the common people felt his merits and his power and the common people of a country are the best feelings of a prophecy of futurity … they are the feelings of nature's sympathies unadulterated with the pretensions of art and pride. They are the veins and arteries that feed and quicken the heart of living fame."[5]

According to the Oxford English Dictionary (OED), celebrity emerged as a word in the seventeenth century meaning "due observance of rites and ceremonies; pomp, solemnity" (OED 1), "a solemn rite or ceremony, a celebration" (OED 2) and "the condition of being much extolled or talked about; famousness, notoriety" (OED 3).

OED 1 is obsolete and OED 4, "a person of celebrity; a celebrated person; a public character" emerged in the mid-nineteenth century with a reference in Miss Mulock's novel *The Ogilvies* (1849).

To attempt a definition, poetic celebrity can be read as a historical-cultural structure involving relations between a poetic self, the publishing industry and audience that impact upon public life. Lord Byron's public persona of "being mad, bad and dangerous to know" was intricately bound up with people reading his actions as if he were one of own poetic heroes. He was the subject of constant newspaper speculation. People would study his engraved portraits for clues to his inner self. By writing about the condition of Europe at a time of

Letter 12: Poetry and Celebrity

Revolution he helped popularise the idea that liberty was a universal ideal. He was seen to lead by example, as John Clare thought when he wanted to return to "his two wives". Opposition to tyrannical government, and numerous radical artisans and printers publishing cheap editions of his work, fed the enormous popularity of Byron, the popular hero.[6] William Wordsworth might have had more lasting impact upon English poetry and life than either Byron and Tennyson but his public persona was lesser than theirs.

To sharpen our working definition of poetic celebrity, let us say that it is a collaborative social process involving a self interacting with an audience through the publishing industry and other media. Byron certainly used his overnight fame for artistic, social and political ends and interacted with his own celebrity whilst building it at the same time. Whereas Barry MacSweeney, notwithstanding the different historical and social situation, by not collaborating with the development of his celebrity after 1968, did not develop a public persona. Echoes of his brush with celebrity and the blurring between public and private occur throughout his work. His fascination with the figure of "celebrity" can be seen in part in his admiration of Thomas Chatterton[7] and Anne Sexton, and some of his late poems, such as 'Postcards from Hitler' (1999)[8] and the 'Mary Bell Sonnets',[9] address the relationship between confession, psychic disturbance and publicity. His own death produced some lurid journalism emphasising his drunkenness and long fall from stardom.[10] MacSweeney's interest is in precisely the direction that his work did take outside of the public arena.

Byron's celebrity in London built upon the example and experience of Mary Robinson (1757–1800), a relatively neglected figure in the twentieth century and the subject of three recent biographies.[11] Feminist scholars began resurrecting Robinson's life and career in the 1990s, when identity and celebrity were becoming key cultural words. This was also the time when the term, "celebrity novelist", was coined.

Robinson's first book of poetry, *Poems* (1775), written in Fleet Prison to get herself out of debt, gained her access to Georgiana, Duchess of Devonshire, and the social 'ton'. Her flamboyant free spirit, her portrayal of Perdita in David Garrick's adaptation of Shakespeare's *The Winter's Tale* at the Theatre Royal, Drury Lane, her subsequent

Letter 12: Poetry and Celebrity

affairs with the Prince of Wales and politicians, her career as a courtesan and ability to use the press to her own advantage, all led to the creation of an intriguing and fascinating personality. She used public knowledge of her exploits for her own ends, and to reinvent herself as a courtesan, and then as a writer. She became a popular Gothic novelist and poet. Her outstanding beauty was much talked and written about. This was surely a reason for Sheridan employing her as an actress and bringing Garrick out of retirement to tutor her. Her complexity and beauty were such that Thomas Gainsborough, who painted her in 1781 and Joshua Reynolds, who painted her as Perdita in 1782, were both criticised for failing to do her justice. Her choice of clothing, increasingly risk-taking, was also much discussed, thus adding to her enigma and allure. She was, like Byron, on the radical wing of the Whigs, welcoming the French Revolution, and active in politics. By 1796 her friends included William Godwin and Mary Wollstonecraft, whose views on marriage, sexuality, slavery and education, she shared. Her sonnet sequence, *Sappho and Phaon* (1796), and pamphlet, *A Letter to the Women of England, on the Injustice of Mental Subordination* (1799), were read and studied by intellectuals. In the preface to *Sappho and Phaon*, she pointedly noted that Sappho's readership idolised the Muse and not the woman. In 1799 she became poetry editor of *The Morning Post*, a newspaper that had written about her since 1775, publishing Wordsworth and Coleridge. Her *Lyrical Tales* (1800), "written in the manner of Wordsworth's Lyrical Ballads" and poems such as, 'The Haunted Beach', which inspired Wordsworth, and 'Golfre', with its echoes of Coleridge's 'Ancient Mariner', are now accepted as part of the early Romantic movement. Her literary relationship with Coleridge is the subject of ongoing research and debate. The journal, *Women's Writing* devoted a special issue (Vol. 9, No.1, 2002) to her work.

Whilst Robinson's Gothic novels and poetry were best-sellers amongst the aristocratic 'ton', her audience was not as large or as socially diverse as Byron's. The emergence of poetic celebrity is linked to the growth of the number of London newspapers from 12 in 1720 to 52 in 1820. There are dozens of references to Perdita and Robinson in many newspapers from the 1780s onwards.[12] After 1774, the end of perpetual copyright allowed a growth in book production and increased readership. Byron's celebrity is more linked to advances in printing technologies between 1785 and 1815, when presses could make 1100 impressions per minute and print both sides of a sheet, and the fact that he allowed cheaper editions of his work to be published in large numbers. There was a similar growth in the reproduction of engraved portraits.[13] This was also the period when journals began to be selective about what they reviewed and more books appeared with the author's name than ever before. It is in this period that the author's name becomes linked with publicity and promotion as with Mary Robinson in *The Morning Post*. There were other short-lived poetry celebrities, such Letitia Landon (1802–1838), promoted as L.E.L in the *Literary Gazette* and invariably associated with vague sexual scandals, Anne Yearsley (1753–1806), promoted as the "milkmaid poet of Bristol" and James Woodhouse, the shoemaker poet.[14] Byron, Robinson and Landon aroused sexual tension and interest. Reading their works and studying their portraits became associated with intimacy and gaining access to their underlying identity. Byron, above all, was able to use that intense interest following the overnight success of *Childe Harold's Pilgrimage* (1812), especially in his epic satire, *Don Juan* (1819–24), with its subtle play around the theme of identity that appealed to his female following, and attack on social and sexual hypocrisy that appealed to his radical support. This work, more than any other in Europe, became associated with personal freedom. *Don Juan*, according to William St Clair in *The Reading Nation in the Romantic Period* (CUP 2005), was read by more people than any previous work of English literature, thanks to cheap pirate editions produced by radical London publishers such as William Benbow, William Hone, Richard Carlile, William Sherwin and William Dugdale. They also published Shelley's *Queen Mab*, Robert Southey's *Wat Tyler,* and other works useful to the libertarian reform movement, in great numbers. *Don Juan* and *The Corsair* (1814) were available in many abbreviated and cheap editions. The pirate editions of the scandalous Harem cantos of *Don Juan* were also integrally involved in the emergence of the obscene press as well as the underground radical press. *The Corsair* sold 10,000 copies on the day of its publication and, like *Don Juan*, exceeded 100,000 sales in all editions.[15]

One of the key aspects of Byron's poetic identity is that it each new instalment of *Childe Harold* and *Don Juan* added to his celebrity

Letter 12: Poetry and Celebrity

by creating a new ingredient to his life story. This satisfied his female followers, who wanted to know more about the man that seemingly challenged and broke social taboos. When *Don Juan* attacked the hypocrisy of married life, it raised the level of mystery and sexual titillation to a higher level, and made Byron's private life the object of intense speculation. The Thomas Phillips portraits of 1814 added to the possibility that Byron was writing about his own life and inner self. By June 1818 reviewers such as John Wilson in the *Edinburgh Review* were convinced that the poet was writing about his private self "as secrets whispered to chosen ears". Byron, though, became aware of the marketing around his work and offers the beginnings of a critique of poetic celebrity. *Don Juan* rejects belief in orderly developmental subjectivity and the narrator refuses notions of a unified self, preferring to be contradictory and inconsistent. "So that I almost think that the same skin / For one without – has two or three within" (Canto 17, 11).

By highlighting marginalised individuals and their social setbacks, culminating in punishment and social marking, *Don Juan* draws attention to the cultural uses of developmental subjectivity as a source of power reliant upon the incremental story of a self's development.[16]

The marketing process needs poetic personae that are in some way fascinating, difficult or controversial. It calls for critics to occupy subject positions in relation to the celebrity poet's behaviour as in the example of Ted Hughes in relation to the suicides of Sylvia Plath and Assia Wevill. Hughes was left with little room to manoeuvre away from such speculation and pointedly did not use his position as Poet Laureate to illuminate his past. Indeed, he gave the impression that he was somewhat indifferent to the Laureateship and wanted to keep his private space, thus adding to his allure. More recent revelations of extramarital affairs have added to his fascination and continued to blur the poet's private and public personae.

In recent times, then, the celebrity poet has become a commodity with a distinct and carefully arranged poetic persona, an intimacy with a possible self. This is reinforced in the criticism, biographies, documentaries and films of the celebrity, adding to the mystery and fascination of the poet. This commoditisation involves critics defending or accusing the situation and persona of a particular celebrity poet and pays dividends when the poet collaborates, as in the recent example of

Letter 12: Poetry and Celebrity

Ted Hughes's *Birthday Letters* (1998), which sold more than 150,000 copies in the first year of its publication.[17]

However it is necessary to read beneath this process and to research the history of the construction of the poetic persona. Dylan Thomas, who emerged as a public figure through his Forties radio broadcasts and the impact of *Under Milk Wood*, a radio play for voices broadcast two months after his premature death in November 1953 in New York, was promoted in a way that emphasised his simpler work and heavy drinking. Thomas's literary executors held quite different poetic ideals to those of the poet and were well prepared to lessen his anti-Movement tendencies in any ways they could. James Nashold and George Tremlett have started work on the exposure of the myth of Thomas's heavy drinking in their book *The Death of Dylan Thomas*[18] but we are still in the strange situation where understanding of his poetic impact has been lessened, and he almost appears a forgotten figure.

R.S. Thomas (1913–2000) cultivated an austere figure as a Welsh poet-priest in remote parts of north Wales writing about Welsh-speaking, Nonconformist hill farmers. His early work from *The Stones of the Fields* (1946) focussed on the starkness of farm labourer's lives and the narrator's feelings for Wales, albeit a Wales of the historical imagination. He wrote of the hill farmers at a distance from their real conditions, their speech and wit, and seemingly wanted them to return to some pre-technological idyll. From *H'm* (1972) onwards, his work is also concerned with an apprehension of God, who is seen as an absence, "the empty silence within", and the concepts of space and time. His final work is concerned with trying to find a meaning for existence and is characterised by some stunning poems about the death of his wife, and their relationship. The poem 'Golden Wedding' acknowledges that "vows are contracted / in the tongue's absence" and admits that it was a marriage not based on romantic love; "over fifty long years / of held breath / the heart has become warm."[19]

After his wife's death, the narrator recognises "a tremor / of light" and looks "up in recognition / of a presence in absence" going "her way" and leaving a scent "which is that of time immolating itself in love's fire."[20] It is the underlying coldness of the relationship that shocks and raises questions about Thomas' calculating personality.

Thomas attacked modern urban life, especially technology, the English encroaching into Wales, and the Welsh responsible for the decay of their own culture and language. He preached to his congregation on the evils of fridges, washing machines and televisions. His anti-consumerism was linked to the loss of God and the worship of wealth and physical comfort instead of finding fulfilment elsewhere. His late books sold more than 20,000 copies each, with poems that have an immediate emotional impact, and through their simplicity resonate quietly. In films, photographs, interviews and poems, he appears to be an extreme Welshman. Indeed he wrote an autobiographical essay where he described himself as "a Welsh-speaking Welshman in a thoroughly Welsh environment."

He was, in fact, as Byron Rogers' biography[21] shows, a Holyhead man who spoke English without a trace of a Welsh accent, who married an English woman and sent his son to an English boarding school. He spoke with all the coldness of an English bureaucrat, and was an outsider to the Welshness that his early poetry seems to espouse, and to the Welsh poetic tradition. Although a priest, he was neither devoted to his parishioners nor was he charitable. His poems indicate that he didn't like Welsh clergymen either. He even introduced the Aberdaron youth club to croquet, the sport of English colonialists. He was such an extreme Welsh nationalist that he could not support Plaid Cymru because it recognised the English parliament. Instead, he publicly supported the Sons of Glendower, who took their name from Owen Glendower, a fifteenth-century Welsh rebel leader. This group led an arsonist campaign against English-owned property in Wales throughout the Eighties. They blamed the influx of middle-class English people, who were taking advantage of cheap Welsh homes at the time of a property boom in southeast England, for diluting the Welsh language and culture and inflating house prices beyond the reach of locals. There is a photograph of Thomas as a craggy old man leaning menacingly from the hatch door of a cottage. The implication is that he is a danger to English visitors and yet this same man accepted the Queen's Medal for Poetry and needed an editor to write in Welsh.

Letter 12: Poetry and Celebrity

Notes

[1] See Jonathan Bate, *John Clare: A Biography* London Picador 2003 pp. 266–267 for Clare's experience of Byron's funeral cortége and Tim Chilcott, *A Publisher and His Circle: the Life and Work of John Taylor, Keats' Publisher* London: Routledge & Kegan Paul 1972, Chapter 4 for Clare's relationship with his publisher.

[2] Tim Chilcott Ed., *John Clare The Living Year 1841* Nottingham: Trent Editions 1999 pp.50–51, 37, 55

[3] Marilyn Butler, *Romantics, Rebels & Reactionaries: English Literature and its Background 1760–1830* Oxford: Oxford University Press 1981 pp. 2–3

[4] Fiona MacCarthy, *Byron: Life and Legend* London: Faber & Faber 2003 p.555

[5] Eric Robinson & David Powell Eds., *John Clare By Himself* Manchester: Carcanet Press 1996 p.157

[6] See E.P. Thompson's *The Making of the English Working Class* Harmondsworth: Pelican Books 1968 p.842 and William St Clair, *The Reading Nation in the Romantic Period* Cambridge: Cambridge University Press 2005

[7] Barry MacSweeney, *Wolf Tongue: Selected Poems 1965–2000* Tarset: Bloodaxe Books 2003 p.37

[8] Barry MacSweeney, *Postcards from Hitler* London: Writer's Forum 1999

[9] Barry MacSweeney, 'The Marvellous Sonnets of Mary Bell' *Tears in the Fence* 21 Autumn 1998 pp.5–8

[10] Gordon Burn, 'Message in a bottle' *The Guardian* Thursday 1 June 2000.

[11] Paula Byrne, *Perdita: The Life of Mary Robinson* London: Harper Collins 2004; Hester Davenport. *The Prince's Mistress* Stroud: Sutton 2004; Sarah Gristwood, *Perdita: Royal Mistress, Writer, Romantic* London: Bantam 2005

[12] Paula Byrne, *Perdita* pp. 127–157; Sarah Gristwood, *Perdita* pp.95–96, 148–153, 181–182

[13] William St Clair, *The Reading Nation in the Romantic Period* pp.134–135, 341–343

[14] Tom Mole, *Byron's Romantic Celebrity: Industrial Culture and the Hermeneutic of Intimacy* Basingstoke: Palgrave Macmillan 2007 p.17

[15] William St Clair, *The Reading Nation in the Romantic Period* pp.327–337

[16] Tom Mole, *Byron's Romantic Celebrity* pp.130–153

[17] Randall Stevenson, *The Oxford English Literary History Vol. 12 1960–2000: The Last of England?* Oxford: Oxford University Press 2004 p.267

[18] James Nashold & George Tremlett, *The Death of Dylan Thomas* Edinburgh: Mainstream 1997

Letter 12: Poetry and Celebrity

[19] R.S. Thomas, *Collected Later Poems 1988–2000* Tarset: Bloodaxe Books 2004 p.328
[20] R.S. Thomas, *No Truce with the Furies* Tarset: Bloodaxe Books p.33
[21] Byron Rogers, *The Man Who Went into the West: The Life of R.S. Thomas* London: Aurum 2006

Letter 13: John Kinsella's Anti-Pastoral

John Kinsella teaches at Cambridge University and Kenyon College, and is very much a global poet of place. Born in Perth, Western Australia in 1963, he arrived on the English poetry scene with a thud on the doormat in the form of *Silo: A Pastoral Symphony* (Arc 1997), *Poems 1980–1994* (Bloodaxe 1998) and *The Hunt & other poems* (Bloodaxe 1998). More books followed, and his prolific output was consolidated in *Peripheral Light: Selected and New Poems* (W.W. Norton 2004). Selected and introduced by Harold Bloom, and praised on the back cover by George Steiner, this book was followed by *The New Arcadia: Poems* (W.W. Norton 2005). He has now produced *Disclosed Poetics: Beyond Landscape and Lyricism* (Manchester University Press 2007), which represents his developing critical position.

Kinsella has consistently situated his poetry within the pastoral, yet his critical work is attempting to move beyond that tradition. In essence, there is a tension between his mainstream pastoral work and his more adventurous attempts at what he terms "linguistic disobedience", as exemplified in his work, *Graphology* (Equipage 1997), and a new lyricism. *Disclosed Poetics* is divided into four chapters on the pastoral, landscape and place; spatial lyricism; manifestoes; ageing, loss, recidivism, with some appendices at the end. It is less a study than a series of explorative approaches in notebook form or as he writes "a stretching out of the poetic line" designed to open out discussion on possible ways forward.

I want to examine some of these ideas around the pastoral and anti-pastoral in the context of Kinsella's recent creative and critical work.

Disclosed Poetics is concerned with what constitutes place and why and how we write about it. As he writes, "Landscape is part of time, and the lyric is a representational grounding of time. The singing of a poem, the rhythm and intonation of a poem, are also inseparable. This is a work that out of its disparate parts suggests a synthesis is possible, even desirable, but recognises the decay, pollution, and destruction of not only natural environments but the markers of place itself." He goes on, "The poem is either complicit with, or resistant to, the status quo, the state-sanctioned version of literature that feeds a stultifying nationalist and hierarchical agenda." This is the issue that drives his poetry and poetics and he is able to draw upon experience in Australia, England and America.[1]

Kinsella poses two questions. Can the pastoral have any relevance in the age of factory farming, genetic modification, pesticides and the disenfranchisement of indigenous communities, and can there be a radical pastoral?

His answers are affirmative and involve challenging and dismantling the building blocks of the pastoral's modes of presentation and representation. This linguistic disobedience involves writing within the rural space and the undoing of the mechanics of the pastoral. He cites Wordsworth's 'Michael' poem as marking the break with the pastoral idyll but gives us no history of the subsequent displacement of the pastoral. Instead he concentrates on the Elizabethan court wits' idea of "Arcadia as a playground for aristocratic or land-owning sensibilities" … "firmly grounded in the hierarchies of control—of the divine right" … "and the ladder of authority that entailed using this as a vehicle for Christian hierarchies"[2] and links this with the world-view of chemical companies that claim to improve the pastoral whilst establishing a hierarchy whereby they gain and the consumer and land face health risks. He thus sees the moral side of the Arcadian ideal as continuing through agencies, such as chemical companies, and being vehicles of hierarchy and authority.

This clearly then was the motivation and thinking behind *The New Arcadia,* although of course it has a wider and deeper context.

Pastoral poetry presents an idealized rather than realistic view of rural life. Dating back to the third century BC, when Theocritus wrote his *Idylls* of Sicilian shepherds, the genre deals with rural life. Virgil added a new dimension to the pastoral by making his Latin *Eclogues* a vehicle for social comment, and setting his poems in a beautiful location, Arcadia, a Greek province, where plain speaking and death occurred. The shepherds are depicted with time on their hands and their thoughts turn to the erotic. Themes include love and seduction, mourning, the corruption of the city or court, invocation of the Muse, the purity of country life and complaints. The eclogues of the title are dialogues between shepherds. Arcadia for Virgil is not a heavenly condition but an earthly one.

By the time of the revived fashion for the pastoral during the Tudor and early Stuart period, Arcadia holds within it the prospect of a radical dimension. The English Arcadians were fiercely Protestant, anti-Spanish, anti-Catholic, and attempting to give roles to love, poetry, land and estate management, their own place as a bulwark between an over-arching monarch and the threat of tyranny. This involved attitudes

Letter 13: John Kinsella's Anti-Pastoral

to common law and the protection of ancient customs and statutes and a balance between the crown and court. They saw the manor as the model for the workings of Arcadia on earth. Here the lord needed to love his tenants as the shepherd needed to love his sheep. There was then a sense of honour involved in running a good estate that looked after its local population. This was the way to happiness and perfection. There was though a contradiction to be overcome. There was continuing protest against land enclosure and this radicalism was linked to an understanding in the Old Testament that saw all men as equal in the sight of God. This tension then is the site of the early radical pastoral. So within the writing there has to be space for old English radicalism in the form of the complaint. Thus in Edmund Spenser's *The Shepherdes Calender* (1579), dedicated to Sir Philip Sidney and which sets the template for the English pastoral, there are twelve eclogues, one for each month of the year, written in different metres and including four on love, two laments, one on the neglect of poetry, four allegories and two complaints. The complaint here is a pointer for the Arcadian towards matters that need to be addressed. It represents, as it were, the social tension between the movements from communality to individuality in land arrangements. English Arcadia came from a world in gradual transition from feudalism to capitalism and is such is looking backwards to communal custom as the font of English law in opposition to court corruption. The pastoral complaint is clearly an anti-pastoral convention that transforms the landscape of innocence into one of conflicted experience. This is clearly where Kinsella's work should be placed.

The affectation of rustic life creates a distancing effect that allows the Arcadian poet to step back and criticise the court and comment on deeper matters. A good example is Shakespeare's *As You Like It* (1600), which contrasts court corruption with the idealised Forest of Arden and invites the viewer to meditate on what constitutes natural behaviour, the nature of love and gender, the connections between language and truth and the abuse of language.

The threat of State power during this period is ever present as writers and poets are imprisoned and murdered and there is also the potential threat of the landed aristocracy, the courtier and lord of the manor as alluded to in Shakespeare's 'Sonnet 94'

> They that have power to hurt, and will do none,
> That do not do the thing they most do show,
> Who, moving others, are themselves as stone,
> Unmoved, cold, and to temptation slow: [3]

Performed at Wilton House, the home of Will Herbert and his mother, the Countess of Pembroke, Sidney's sister, in 1603 in front of James I, at a time when Ralegh, a banished courtier like those in *As You Like It*, was imprisoned nearby at Winchester, the play contains echoes of Marlowe's poetry ('The Passionate Shepherd to His Love') and death, as in Touchstone's speech in Act III Scene iii, and with its happy ending perhaps calls on divine intervention in favour of love and goodness from a benevolent lord or monarch. It clearly draws the viewer into another world where characters can try on different identities and this openness and its unresolved debates create the space for the audience to probe. It is one of the best examples of the pastoral process being used to make readers think.

William Empson in *Some Versions of Pastoral* (1935) famously saw the pastoral process of "putting the complex into the simple"[4], and that the pastoral has a unifying social force and is a means of bridging differences and reconciling social classes. In his rapid sketch of the pastoral, Kinsella is against the construction of new pastoral idylls and sees the pastoral as a genre of closure, which perhaps forgets the achievements of *As You Like It*, and yet he also sees that the pastoral has moral, spiritual and gender aspects in our time. In a moving passage, he writes about his teenage years spent shooting and trapping parrots in Western Australia and his writing about parrots, symbol of the destruction of beauty, as an act of atonement. I find that Kinsella is far more effective in this writing than in his unstructured thinking on the pastoral. *Disclosed Poetics* essentially records the progress of his own thinking about the pastoral and linguistic disobedience, making use of his own poems and recent examples of the radical pastoral by Peter Larkin, Andrew Duncan and Lisa Robertson. The spatial lyricism and manifestoes chapters are full of provocative notes and thoughts that draw upon a wide range of recent poetics and theory. However, there is no underlying coherent overall approach, although the possible directions are clear. By implication, he rejects two recent ideas that seem to me to be misleading. One that the pastoral is

Letter 13: John Kinsella's Anti-Pastoral

solely a discourse of retreat and two that its age has ended, as suggested in Terry Gifford's *Pastoral* and elsewhere. He sees the radical pastoral as occupying the fringe areas between the rural and urban and between speech / writing and thought.[5] Although the pastoral is a discourse of ideological accommodation, the anti-pastoral can be read as breaking new ground and making us think anew as Ralegh, Shakespeare, Milton and Courbet, the painter, have shown. I would like to suggest, though, that the response to the pastoral—and that arguably includes the anti-pastoral—is to do its opposite, that is, as Elizabeth Cook has written of my work "to repeatedly unpack the simple to examine the latent complexity of implication and relationship"[6] within the context of a localised and deeper social history.

Coming to *The New Arcadia* after reading *Disclosed Poetics*, it is surprisingly orthodox and simple. Promoted as a response to Sidney's *Old Arcadia* (1580) it employs irony to present the "new" Arcadia not in a "feigned" or fantasy realm but in modern rural Western Australia with all the downsides of rural life being used to present the anti-pastoral.

The *Old Arcadia*, a prose romance with poems and eclogues, is a virtuoso performance of French and Italian forms transposed into English verse. Sidney wrote this way for the music, and passions that the words could excite. The eclogues are largely songs and recitations on such themes as marriage, melancholy and death, presented during singing competitions that provide the pretext for the metrical complexity and experiment introduced by each singer. The work's success is derived from the tension between the formal experiments and thematic exploration involving enormous inventiveness and a full command of English.

The New Arcadia is divided into five acts, each beginning with a narrative poem that provides a temporal snapshot and ending with an eclogue, and employs a range of registers characterised by a modulated musical language. It has a graceful flow with flourishes of higher pitched narration depicting the Avon Valley, east of Perth, beset with unsettling relationships between people, animals, birds and plants.

Compared to the *Old Arcadia*, it is not a dramatic literary construct designed to advance thinking about moral and emotional behaviour. There is plenty of death and invention and a relative lack of love poems. It is written at speed, as if there is a need to cover a wide region rather than a localised space, and consequently the speakers' voices are more neutral than dialect. The lack of rough edges to the poetry somewhat mitigates against seeing this as a true opposite to the *Old Arcadia,* where all the characters portrayed are good poets. The narrator explains that "People measure lives by the miles / they've chewed up" and that there's "a lot of bad poetry here".[7]

The New Arcadia is best seen as anti-pastoral rather than radical pastoral. Anti-pastoral has a long tradition at least going back to Ralegh's 'The Nymphs Reply to the Shepherd' (1600), a satirical riposte to Marlowe's poem 'The Passionate Shepherd to His Love' (1600), and would include Stephen Duck's *The Thresher's Labour* (1736), Mary Collier's reply, *The Woman's Labour: an Epistle to Mr Stephen Duck* (1739). Interestingly, these and other anti-pastoral poems came to be read as pastoral poems, and that may eventually happen to Kinsella's work. Indeed, rather than seeing the touchstone of the break with the pastoral in Wordsworth's 'Michael', there is an alternative tradition provided by Shakespeare's *As You Like It*, Blake's *Songs of Innocence and Experience* (1794), and *The Marriage of Heaven and Hell* (1794), which involves a much different use of language. The anti-pastoral satirical tradition of Ralegh and Milton is relevant to this tradition and I was surprised not to see reference to this work in Kinsella's largely autobiographical chapter on ageing in *Disclosed Poetics*. Briefly, the Arcadian world of conventions and cycles of conflicting judgements about country and city, male and female, and the contrary states of youth, maturity and old age, are brought under great strain from within. As Ralegh says in 'The Nymph's Reply to the Shepherd': "thy beds of roses, / Thy cap, thy kirtle, and thy posies / Soon break, soon wither, soon forgotten, — / In folly ripe, in reason rotten."[8]

It may be then that Ralegh and Milton were interested, as Kinsella is now, in undoing the mechanics of the pastoral from within. However, the anti-pastoral should move forward and explore the tensions and contradictions between the human and non-human, masculine and feminine selves, the country and city, the workings of globalisation as it impacts upon rural economies, landowner and tenant and farm worker, tenant and farm worker.

One of Kinsella's strengths is his eagerness to be open about his various subject positions and an ability to acknowledge his own prejudices. As he writes in *Disclosed Poetics*, "Ploughing a field on Wheatlands when I was eighteen is every bit as important to me as first reading Deleuze and Guattari, and being a vegan as essential as enjoying the poetry of Shelley. In my adult life, the teaching of poetry has become inseparable from my poetics: I teach what and how I have learned so others can learn for themselves. I am interested in offering approaches and processes, not end results. The unfinished intrigues me."[9]

Although his family and farm, Wheatlands, are mentioned in *The New Arcadia*, his exact relationship to the land is not examined or presented. Although it is possible to infer that parents within the range of large landowner to smallholder raised him, the exact conditions and status are excluded. The value of this information is relevant to questions concerning who worked and originally lived on the land.

His 'Eclogue of Presence'[10] does however raise the question of ownership and land access. Here the Farmer says that everything "between river and hills / is mine, / and you need my permission to cross even the / gullies", and the Young Bloke replies that "this scrub is for anyone to walk through, unna?". The Farmer says that he will kill kangaroos that invade his crops and the Young Bloke replies that evening brings a light that shows the dead the way up the hills to "fill the darkness and occupy every noise." The eclogue continues, giving voice to the Farmer and young Aborigine, and effectively contrasts their different views of the land in an unresolved debate. Many other poems, such as 'The Cull', 'Against Conflation' and 'Home', with its barbed-wire image, perform the same function of presenting unresolved tensions and conflicts. A typical example is the poem, 'White Cockatoos', where the birds are seen as raucous spectres "it's said like broken glass" / "field into quadrature out / of blind-spots" and are "ready to turn" their beaks back towards green crops.[11]

Disclosed Poetics provides the poem's context by explaining the role and function of parrots in Australian poetry and culture as political and environmental symbols. The poem plays on the knowledge that white cockatoos are pests that eat crops and fruit and the paradox between its familiarity as an object of splendour and derision. The poem's own acknowledged failure in the "broken glass" simile thus leads to the larger realisation that the poem only partially grasps the actual impact of such birds on the psyche.

Given the way that the pastoral ideology works to incorporate its opposite within its own dialectic, *The New Arcadia*—despite its flourishes in poems such as 'Extreme Conditions Occasion the Fox', 'Dead Wood and Scorpions' and the Reflectors poems—does lack in linguistic disobedience. It is to Kinsella's enormous credit that he has produced a most unusual book that more than questions the foundations of his critically successful poetry.

Notes

[1] John Kinsella, *Disclosed Poetics: Beyond Landscape and Lyricism* Manchester: Manchester University Press 2007 p. xii
[2] Ibid p. 1
[3] William Shakespeare, *The Complete Works* Oxford Shakespeare Head Press / Blackwell 1934 p. 1236. See also J.H. Prynne, *They That Haue Powre To Hurt: A Specimen of a Commentary on Shake-speares Sonnets, 94* Cambridge: privately published 2001
[4] William Empson, *Some Versions of Pastoral* Cambridge: Cambridge University Press 1935 p.23
[5] Terry Gifford, *Pastoral* London: Routledge 1999 p.67
[6] Elizabeth Cook '*Man In Black*: David Caddy' *The Use of English* Vol. 60 No. 2 Summer 2008 pp. 287–291
[7] John Kinsella, *The New Arcadia* New York: W.W. Norton 2005 pp. 4,7
[8] Walter Ralegh, *The Poems of Sir Walter Ralegh* Ed. Agnes Latham London: Routledge & Kegan Paul 1962 p.16. I have modernised the extract.
[9] John Kinsella, *Disclosed Poetics* p. xi
[10] John Kinsella, *The New Arcadia* pp. 96–101
[11] Ibid p. 56

LETTER 14: J.H. PRYNNE

In February 2004, Randall Stevenson writing in *The Oxford English Literary History Vol. 12 1960–2000: The Last of England?*[1] (OUP 2004) inadvertently sparked a media controversy by suggesting that the achievements of experimental poets, such as J.H. Prynne, would be of more lasting significance than that of the Movement poets. The value of J.H. Prynne's poetry was debated in newspapers and on the radio but not seriously engaged with. As I regularly get asked about the value of Prynne's poetry, I thought that I might offer some contextualising notes as a preliminary to reading his *Poems* (Bloodaxe 2005).

The arc of Prynne's poetry over the past forty years may be said to have broadly moved from a metaphorically based open field lyricism towards a metonymic and etymological challenge to the reader. It is, above all, concerned with encouraging the reader on a journey, involving a reading process that avoids closure. It is about the journey, that is a continual process, towards meaning and comprehension rather than finding answers. It places utterance within the political and socio-economic predicament of the individual in relation to its historical and geographical landscape. One might say that it is one journey of utterance that acknowledges the boundaries and thresholds of the individual, through and across the nuances and shifts of language and historical time. It draws upon specific discourses and their appeal to knowledge, both provisional and substantive, within the languages of criticism and human sciences and beyond. It is a poetic utterance that looks back to the earliest epic and founding literature and forward beyond any post-modernist position. It has enlarged the focus of the poet beyond the reference frames registered by Ezra Pound's *The Cantos* and Charles Olson's *The Maximus Poems*. It appeals to a community of speakers, readers and writers, cognizant of the fact that all are in a series of markets and hierarchies of language and discourse outlays, without privilege.

This work is substantially supported by critical essays, such as 'Stars, Tigers and the Shape of Words' (The William Matthews Lectures 1992, Birkbeck 1993), where Prynne reassessed the arbitrariness that Ferdinand de Saussure famously attributed to the signifier and signified and emphasized a set of secondary relations through which meaning developed such as historical contexts and usages, accumulated layers and aspects of association, social function and usage codes, and practical criticism, such as *They That Haue Powre To Hurt: A Specimen of a Commentary on Shake-speares Sonnets, 94* (Cambridge 2001) and *Field Notes: The Solitary Reaper And Others* (Cambridge 2007, distributed by Barque Press) that shows an exceptional regard to determining the fullest context and meaning of a poem. Each word and phrase in a poem has a philological and etymological base that returns the reader to things and the world of which they are a part. The words used enact and sustain the relations and forces between language and the world.

Two words invariably used to describe the initial experience of reading the *Poems* are "arid" and "difficult". "Arid", as if it were written in a desert. That is to say that it is often missing the props of mainstream metaphorical poetry which enable a quick grasp of the meaning, intention and scope of the poem under review. It is what is called "difficult" poetry. It is, as it were, poetry of the desert. I shall now pursue these two notions as a way of locating the literary context to the *Poems*.

Poetry written from the desert, of whatever order, may be seen as poetry of exile. One thinks of Ovid, Paul and Jane Bowles, and the post-Holocaust poetry of Edmond Jabès and Paul Celan. The critic. T.W. Adorno wrote that "after Auschwitz, we can no longer write poetry". It was Jabès who wrote that, after Auschwitz, "we *must* write poetry, but with wounded words" and who said, in conversation with Mark C Taylor: "It is very hard to live with silence. The real silence is death and this is terrible. To approach this silence, it is necessary to journey into the desert. You do not go into the desert to find identity, but to lose it, to lose your personality, to become anonymous. You make yourself void. You become silence. And something extraordinary happens: you hear silence speak".[2] Further, poetry of exile or of self-imposed exile has a social position and literary effect. By dint of being outside the social-literary mainstream, it is more able to comment inwards on the prevailing socio-political conditions. One thinks of Anna Akhmatova's ability to comment in her poetry upon Stalinist Russia and the purges. Prynne's poetry, like Jabès and Akhmatova, may be seen in broad moral and literary terms as a profound reaction to the historic events of the twentieth century and beyond.

J.H. Prynne's socio-literary position can be seen as one of self-imposed exile. He has been, for example, excluded from such literary reference books as *The Oxford Companion to English Literature*, edited by Margaret Drabble (OUP 2000) and taken moral decisions on the integrity of how and where his poetry and criticism appears.

Letter 14: J.H. Prynne

His exact socio-literary position is complex, given its predominantly exile status. Born in 1936, Jeremy Prynne was raised in Kent and educated at Jesus College, Cambridge. His mother ran a private nursery school for boys and girls and his father was an engineer. At Cambridge he met the poet and critic, Donald Davie, who supported his early intellectual direction. In common with Davie, this constituted a move away from the insular concerns of the Movement to the richer intellectual concerns of new American and European poetry. Davie's study, *Thomas Hardy and Modern Poetry* (1973) offers an early account of Prynne's poetry. A Life Fellow, College Librarian and University Reader in English Poetry until his retirement at Gonville and Caius College, Cambridge, he works on all aspects of the English poetic tradition, as well as writings of American, European and Far Eastern origin. In his teaching capacity, his enthusiasm for sharing, and his generosity of spirit towards many students, is well known and has helped to develop a wide readership base. However, this is only part of the story. Prynne's poetry emerged as part of an avant-garde discussion and readership outside the literary marketplace. This began with Prynne's editorship of *Prospect* magazine in 1964 and continued with his mimeographing and distributing *The English Intelligencer*, a literary newsletter, between January 1966 and April 1968.

The English Intelligencer was an attempt to organise a new collective poetics that focussed upon the production of "quality" work. Drawing upon a wide range of literary and non-literary sources, it was distributed free to an expanding mailing list. Poems, essays and comments were shared without cost or exchange value. *The Intelligencer* occupied a space between a private letter and public book and embodied a shared community opposition to market commodification.

J.H. Prynne was a key figure in its articulation of the language and poetics of "quality" in opposition to the language of commodity. Essentially, he wanted to rescue a concept of "quality" from its financial meaning to make it viable outside a purely market lexicon. In the poem, 'Sketch for a Financial Theory of the Self' (*Poems* pp.19–20), which first appeared Series 1 no. 17, Prynne probes the relationship between word (name) and object within the economic field and suggests the ways in which it impacts on the self. He writes of how words and poems and quality, as habit, have been reduced to monetary objects by which we define ourselves. He notes that we are duped into a reductive cash flow nexus: "The absurd trust in value is the pattern of / bond and contract and interest" and "Music, / travel, habit and silence are all money; purity / is a glissade into the last, most beautiful return." He extended his thinking on quality and money with 'A Note on Metal' (*The English Intelligencer*, second series, June 1967, and reprinted as an appendix to *Aristeas* (1968)).[3] Here, quality is seen in terms of property (strength) and substance. He looks back to the origins of money as coin (gold) and Western alchemy, defined as "the theory of quality as essential". He differentiates between early Asiatic socio-economic formations, where coins were the ornament of power rather than currency of value, and early Greek economies where it is the substance governing transfer as exchange. This thinking is brought historically up to date in the poem, 'Die a Millionaire' from *Kitchen Poems* (1968), where the "twist-point / is 'purchase'—what the mind / bites on is yours" ... "we are the social strand / which is already past the twist-point & / into the furnace" ... "so that what I am is a special case of / what we want, the twist-point missed exactly / at the nation's scrawny neck."[4]

The English Intelligencer, by removing formal ownership and exchange value, produced a newsletter divorced from the literary market. In so doing, they showed that words and poems, as objects, have properties beyond their meanings and exchange value within the community. This move can be seen as an extension of the work and thinking of the Objectivist poets, such as George Oppen, Charles Reznikoff and Louis Zukofsky, who searched for a language outside the ideology and practice of commodification.

The English Intelligencer fostered intense interest in a wide range of poetries and philosophy. These included Ezra Pound and the Imagists, William Carlos Williams and the poetry of things, the Objectivist poets, the Black Mountain College poets, the San Francisco Renaissance, the New York School poets, such as Frank O'Hara and John Ashbery, and the European post-Holocaust poets, such as Jabès and Celan. Beyond that widening flux of alternative poetries, Prynne continued his readings within the English tradition, especially the Romantic and Elizabethan poets, and within modern European philosophy, including Hegel, Wittgenstein, Heidegger, Merleau-Ponty, and the issues of language, being and the phenomenology of perception raised by their work.

Letter 14: J.H. Prynne

Amongst the questions that this reading raised would be the notion of the autonomy of the text and whether there is a singleness and moral structure to immediate knowledge.[5]

The historical backdrop to *The English Intelligencer* saw growing disenchantment with the Vietnam War, civil disobedience for women's, gay and environmental issues, industrial strife, a balance-of-trade deficit that led to the devaluation of the pound, and students "revolt into style" on the streets. Inside universities, the concept of the de-centred subject and the de-centring structure had spread from structuralism—its origins in linguistics and anthropology—throughout the human sciences within Europe. Doubtless buoyed by E.P. Thompson's articulation of the impact of literary, satirical and political presses in the early nineteenth century in *The Making of the English Working Class* (1968) and Jeff Nuttall's overview of more recent oppositional publishing and culture in *Bomb Culture* (1968), several contributors to *English Intelligencer* became small press publishers. It was through these regional activists that J.H. Prynne chose to publish most of his early work. (e.g. *Day Light Songs*: Resuscitator Books, Pampisford 1968; *Aristeas*: Ferry Press, London 1968; *The White Stones*: Grosseteste Review Press, Lincoln 1969; and *Fire Lizard*: Blacksuede Boot Press, Barnet 1970).

Prynne's early readership, then, consisted of friends, the avant-garde poets, intellectuals and critics associated with *The English Intelligencer*, his colleagues and students. The nature of his communication with that growing audience took the form of his poetry and a contribution to the thinking and reading of that audience. It is a literary-social position in relation to a mode of poetic creation that involves questioning before and beyond any current ideology of text, authorship, intention and marketing process. It entails, as a reader and poet, a wandering across and through both language and the literary canon. Over time he deepens and widens that range, by attempting not to suppress variable meaning and knowledge that impinge upon a thing, so that the reader might question various knowledge thresholds, in particular such concepts as "totality", "immediate experience" and "textual autonomy".

Turning to the notion of "difficulty": this familiar notion in the poetry world is encountered in the first line of the first poem, the magically sonic, 'The Numbers': "The whole thing it is, the difficult". A note to the 1982 edition of *Poems* (Allardyce, Barnett, Publishers) referred to "difficulty as being the ardent matter and accompanying breadth of imaginative and political reference". In other words, it is inherent in the matter addressed as the forces and relations of production and consumption already taint the nuances of languages and knowledge. There is no impartial discourse. "Difficulty", though, is not misleading, that is to say, the reader is either able to grasp something or not. It perhaps implies that the conflicting and impartial knowledge at work is beyond the reach of one reader and some of these poems are beyond comprehension, through the uncertainty of variable meaning. However, it should be seen, at least, as relative, and in relation to "simplicity". A seemingly transparent and simple poem, such as Blake's 'The Tyger', may require considerable critical work in disentangling the complexity of discourses, method and intentionality, and possible effects registered, in the same way as a "difficult" poem, given that so much of its subtext is out of view. This can perhaps be described as "subtlety" in all its guises. Both "difficult" and "simple" poems demand intellectual work and are initially conditioned by prejudicial readings and the disposition towards response and effect. In other words, some poems produce effects and reference knowledge that are unseen or unread by certain readers and that is governed by reading history and preferences as much as ability of the reader. An awareness of that history, conditioned as it is by ethnic, social, educational, psychological and other factors, and its prejudice, may help dissolve some of the weariness generated by poems that refuse to be read. At the macro-level, it might help reader appreciate the divide between those who read poems as language only and those who read poems as social process only and show the need to resist closure on either side of the fence. "Difficulty" can be distinguished from "subtlety", meaning that which is not obvious in any way, possessing small and important data, often implying cleverness through its ability to withhold and disguise. Subtlety, then, wants to be acknowledged rather than seen. Difficulty, in contrast, has intrinsic value in the sense that a poem retains its vitality over time, as in the case of Wordsworth's 'Lucy' poems, and implies an openness or opening towards the complex. It is potentially much less elitist than a work of subtlety.

Letter 14: J.H. Prynne

The arc of Prynne's poetry may be seen as moving further into exile, a deepening of the challenge to the reader, as a method of registering wider referents, on the basis that might be a focal point of social and ethical or literary change. Consider the examples of Blake and Kafka, as psychological exiles, self-imposed or not, and the ways their work has entered the language. Now consider, at the micro-level, the individual forced by exceptional circumstances, e.g. the loss of several high school friends to suicide, into self-imposed exile, who returns and begins to campaign for social change. Consider also a woman who is sexually abused, attacked and raped or the female vagrant. This is the possible territory called into reference by *Her Weasels Wild Returning* (1994),[6] where there are a series of explicit journeys out and back by the poem's implied participants. What happens in these examples is a journey out to exile and a journey back, in altered state, with its concomitant changes. Of course, the exiled do not return to exactly the same place, as time has elapsed since they left. In a way this is akin to the experience of reading Prynne's poetry.

Interestingly Prynne has spoken of a poetry that journeys out and back. It is a poetic and critical example that clearly informs Prynne's method of composition and reading. Prynne reads Charles Olson's *Maximus Poems IV, V, VI* as having set "the literal founding of history and its local cadence into speech extend outwards by feeling into the sacral and divinised forms of presence upon the earth's surface" and established as primary writing, "with a lingual and temporal syncretism, poised to make a new order". In other words it places language as a mythological likeness resting on the earth through geological time and the *monogene* which "reaches back into two entwined histories: the geochronology of land-formation and cytochronology of biochemical evolution".[7]

In his 1971 Simon Fraser University lectures on *The Maximus Poems IV, V, VI*, Prynne equates the homecoming of Maximus with the homecoming of *The Odyssey* and argues that the poem brings in the cosmos, that is knowledge of the universe considered as whole. At the beginning of *Maximus IV, V, VI* the narrative turns back from the sea, by which the narrator, for Prynne, means space and the large condition of the cosmos. For Olson to look from the Gloucester coast out into the Atlantic is to look into the whole economic support of early New England settlement and to look back to the mid-Atlantic ridges, that is to the residues of the birth of the earth. Olson, then, has an outward journey and inward journey, stretching lyricism into epic through the folding back of the voyage out. Prynne argues that each of the *Maximus* fragments participates in the whole, so that it is literal and not an insistence of something else and thus escapes metaphor. As such, this leads to a condition of being which is beyond the condition of meaning. The arc of the *Maximus Poems* is a singular journey, to the limits of space and back to local historical roots, achieved as a curvature that moves beyond the lyric into the condition of myth.[8]

Olson provided Prynne with a modern epic template, of the journey out and back, and of poetry that places language on earth in geophysical time through the monogene. Prynne has extended this model into a reading experience that is uniquely his own, redolent with acute vocabularies and terse energy points. He offers encounters with language and the various discourses that impinge upon the individual showing how the individual is formed by processes that are outside immediate perception and cognition. His movement beyond metaphorical language seems to be entirely consistent with the scope of his initial enquiries and an attempt to find a more adequate measure of discursive pressures. Recurrent figures and sound patterns replace normative narratives. The use of juxtaposition and enjambment to move seamlessly from one thought or perception to another is done, as Olson advised in his 1950 'Projective Verse' essay, at speed so as to bring seemingly disparate discourses, or elements of discourses, into the sphere of activity being registered. Olson's impact on Prynne is most noticeable in his early work, especially *The White Stones*, which can be read, in part, as an investigation of the transfer of language to the human account. It is Olson's 1959 'Human Universe' essay that forms a backbone to the collection's frame of reference. In this essay Olson saw all post-Socratic philosophy as a false discourse of logic, classification and idealism, as opposed to a discourse that takes language as an action upon the real. "We have lived long in a generalizing time, at least since 450BC", he wrote, and went on to distinguish between "language as the act of the instant and language as the act of thought about the instant".[9]

To Olson, Aristotelian logic and classification have fastened themselves on habits of thought, so that action is absolutely interfered with. In other words, habits of thought are habits of action, collapsing

Letter 14: J.H. Prynne

language from an instrument into an absolute, with the Greeks declaring all speculation as enclosed in the "universe of discourse". Olson calls for a writing that does not fall back "on the dodges of discourse", a demonstration, a separating out, a classification. "For any of us, at any instant, are juxtaposed to any experience, even an overwhelming single one, on several more planes than the arbitrary and discursive which we inherit can declare".[10] This could surely stand as a preface to the work of Prynne's *Poems*. Olson further notes that a thing impinges upon us by self-existence, without reference to any other thing, by its particularity that is to be found beyond reference and description, and wants to bear in rather than away from a thing, so as to discover and reveal.

Olson's *Maximus* and the 'Human Universe' essay, combined with Homer's epic *The Odyssey*, leads Prynne and the reader to consider exile in terms of the founding moment of historical self-awareness and, at the same time, as the site of various philosophical and individual splits and boundaries. It is the exile posited on the material foundation of historical change or reinstatement and displaced from any singular viewpoint. By challenging our ordinary linguistic ordering of the world, beginning with an analysis of concept formation in the financial world, Prynne's poetry makes us question the way in which we make sense of things.

Letter 14: J.H. Prynne

Notes

[1] Randall Stephenson. *The Oxford English Literary History Vol. 12 1960–2000: The Last of England?* Oxford: Oxford University Press 2004 pp. 229, 234–236, 270
[2] Edmond Jabès. *The Book of Margins*: Translated by Rosemarie Waldrop Chicago: University of Chicago Press 1993
[3] J.H. Prynne. *Poems* Tarset: Bloodaxe Books 2005 pp.127–132
[4] Ibid pp.13–16
[5] For a discussion of these issues see Kevin Nolan 'Capital Calves: Undertaking an Overview' *Jacket* 24 November 2003, viewable at www.jacket.com pp. 1–37
[6] J.H. Prynne. *Poems* pp. 412–416
[7] J. H. Prynne. 'Charles Olson, *Maximus Poems IV, V, VI*' *The Park* 4 & 5 Summer 1969 pp. 64–66
[8] *Minutes of the Charles Olson Society* No 28 April 1999 pp. 3–13. www.charlesolson.ca/files/Prynnelecture
[9] Ralph Maud Ed. *A Charles Olson Reader* Manchester: Carcanet Press 2005 p. 113
[10] Ibid p. 114

Letter 15: Andrew Crozier

In my last talk I mentioned J.H. Prynne's contribution to *The English Intelligencer*. I would now like to say a few words about literary connection in the context of Andrew Crozier, who collated and edited the first series of *The English Intelligencer*. Crozier, who died in April 2008, is a much less well-known figure than he might be and left a substantial and lasting legacy as a poet, editor and teacher. He was instrumental in recovering some of the forgotten history of Modernism through his retrieval of the works of John Rodker,[1] J.F Hendry[2] and others.[3]

The idea of literary connection is full of potential difficulty and complication as we lack words for the different types of relationships and connections. Moreover critics tend to label poets together by dint of association, and essential differences can be lost. Connection is closely attached to selling a particular poet or book, regardless of whether an underlying connection exists or not and again can be used loosely.

Literary connection is also associated with place and tourism. Thus, Derbyshire and the Peak District advertise their connection with the Elizabethan historian, William Camden, who wrote about the "Wonders of the Peak" in *Britannia* (1586), and other writers and poets throughout the centuries. Camden's work, of course, was central in forming the concept of a unified nation. The Peaks are sufficiently distinctive and attractive to become part of the national identity, and the issues around its constitution, so that they are at once local, regional and national, as reinforced by Thomas Hobbes in his poem *De Mirabilibus Pecci* (1636) which celebrated Chatsworth House, Peak Cavern, St Anne's Well, Buxton, Eldon Hole and Tideswell. The Peak District is the locus of Crozier's friend—and editor of the second series of *The English Intelligencer*—Peter Riley's *Tracks and Mineshafts* (Grosseteste 1983; republished in *The Derbyshire Poems*, Shearsman Books 2010). A work that meditates on the significance of "abandoned mines, standing out like sores through the rough mingling pastoral surface"[4] and engages with Seventies cultural politics through a reading of the ideology of English landscape poetry and insists on digging deeper into "the message that exceeds us, the concept not grasped, the emptiness of total being, pure sign of itself to which such substances as metal, poetry, history, can only be tools of an interim script".[5]

Connection, the action of connecting or joining together (OED 1a) was first used in the 1609 edition of the Bible. From Thomas Hobbes in *Leviathan* (1651) we have (OED 1b) of immaterial union or joining together and (OED 2a) the linking together of words or ideas in speech or thought. From the base of the action or condition of being joined together the idea of connection has been added so that it has eleven meanings that cover links without specification. There is a gap in the English language that allows a simple notion of linkage to be employed that denies individuality and difference in favour of easy labelling and obfuscation. Smaller and deeper underlying contextual links are often unread and dormant as a result.

Issues around national identity, what constitutes "Englishness" and whether we should have connections with foreign poets and poetry have dominated the struggles within English poetry since the 1900s especially between Modernism and the Movement and their successors and reaching a crisis from 1956 to 1963 and subsequent battle during the mid-1970s.[6] Thus Robert Conquest in his introduction to *New Lines–II* (1963) could write of a return to the cardinal traditions of English verse and warn against poetry that is written from new or different attitudes and state that "the human condition from which the poetry of one country springs cannot be readily tapped by that of another."[7]

In 1961 Andrew Crozier won an exhibition to Christ's College, Cambridge to read English, having won a scholarship to Dulwich College, south east London in 1954. He was arrested twice for civil disobedience on the Campaign for Nuclear Disarmament's Aldermaston demonstrations. As an undergraduate, Crozier edited an American supplement to *Granta* magazine and included work by Robert Duncan, Edward Dorn, Robert Creeley and John Wieners. At the end of this publishing adventure, which was prepared to rattle the status of the Movement poets, he added a letter from Charles Olson to George Butterick that included the phrase "freshen our sense of the language we do have" adding that the "spirit of Olson informs this whole collection".

Amongst his friends were the American poet and *The Paris Review* poetry editor, Tom Clark, studying English at Gonville and Caius on a Fulbright Scholarship, who would later write critical biographies of Ted Berrigan, Jack Kerouac, Robert Creeley, Charles Olson and Edward Dorn, as well as John Temple, Peter Riley and John Riley, with whom his work shares an affinity.[8]

In 1964 he studied at the State University of New York, Buffalo, on a Fulbright Scholarship, publishing the broadsheet series *Sum* and the journal, *The Ant's Forefoot*, and was tutored by Charles Olson. Whilst in America, Crozier contacted the Objectivist poet, Carl Rakosi, who had changed his name to Callman Rawley and stopped writing. Rakosi later acknowledged that Crozier's determination to find him had persuaded him to return to writing poetry. Crozier's discovery of Rakosi led to a much wider awareness of the Objectivists. The impact of Olson on Crozier's thought can be gauged by the use of a line from Olson as the title for his Collected Poems: *All Where Each Is* (Agneau 2, Allardyce, Barnett 1985).

On returning to London in January 1966, Crozier began *The English Intelligencer* before joining Donald Davie at Essex University, where he wrote his doctoral thesis, *Free Verse as Formal Restraint*, and founded *The Wivenhoe Park Review* with Tom Clark. This in turn became *The Park* when he moved to teach at Keele University in 1967. J.H. Prynne's introduction to Crozier's first book of poetry, *Loved Litter of Time Spent* (1967) refers to a central quality in the writing 'the possible as it really comes over, day by day'.[9]

The English Intelligencer rejected the received modes of established Movement poetics in favour of a new, modernist poetics of diversity that shifted attention away from the insular towards a broader field of activity. The newsletter was distributed free to interested individuals and encouraged an open forum for exchange, and was clearly looking to develop a new English poetics. Crozier insisted early on that 'the *Intelligencer* is for the island and its language, to circulate as quickly as needs be.'[10] This is curious language. "The *Intelligencer* is for the island and its language". The immediate context of this statement is the Movement's wholesale rewriting of the history of modern poetry, and the suppression of part of that history, and its claims to speak for the nation. Donald Davie, one of the theorists of the Movement, famously wrote in *Granta* 68 in 1963 that "everyone knows, really, that Philip Larkin is the effective laureate of our England", annexing poetic quality and national culture in an uncomplicated and empirical alignment. The thrust of this annexing and suppression was reinforced in polemical anthologies and histories, such as Robert Conquest's *New Lines–II* (Macmillan 1963), Blake Morrison's *The Movement: English Poetry and Fiction in the Fifties* (OUP 1980), Al Alvarez's *The New Poetry* (Penguin

1966) and Blake Morrison and Andrew Motion's *The Penguin Book of Contemporary British Poetry* (Penguin 1982). Crozier brought a return to what Robert Conquest in his 1956 *New Lines* anthology wanted to remove from English poetry that is to say, intellect, strong emotion and "social pressure". Crozier brought intellectual rigour to his editorial work as explained by an early contributor, Chris Torrance, in a private conversation in March 2006. It was Crozier's advice and support that led Torrance to Olson and the much wider world of American music, painting and writing.

Through Torrance's work and teaching one can follow the Olson line to a new generation of contemporary poets such as Elisabeth Bletsoe and Rhys Trimble.

Crozier founded Ferry Press in London in 1964, first publishing *Thread* by Fielding Dawson, the painter and poet, who had studied at Black Mountain College. The Press became, with John Riley and Tim Longville's *Grosseteste Review*, an important outlet for J.H. Prynne, Peter Riley, John James, John Hall, John Temple, Chris Torrance, Douglas Oliver, Wendy Mulford and others who had contributed to *The English Intelligencer*. This connection, however much forgotten or ignored, is real enough. That many of the poets involved lived and worked in Cambridge is also undeniable, but not particularly useful to know until you question their social and work situation. Moreover, Crozier and his friends were frequent visitors to London in the mid-Sixties and in particular, Better Books, where the poets, Bob Cobbing and Lee Harwood worked, and a lot of networking and readings took place. The frequent denial of a so-called Cambridge School has much to do with an understanding of connection and process. Yes, Cambridge is an early focus point but so is Better Books, and later, Compendium Books, and Essex University. The denial can be read therefore as a deflection to persuade the reader to look deeper. The document that most clearly articulates Crozier's position is his introduction, written with Tim Longville, to the anthology *A Various Art*.[11]

Here the introduction emphasised "the degree of difference that existed between individual poets, and the extent to which each poet had accomplished a characteristic and integral body of work, with its own field of interest and attention,' and claimed 'both the possibility and presence of such variety, a poetry deployed towards the complex and multiple experience in language of all of us."[12] It is noteworthy for refusing any collective stance, its advocacy of diversity and for producing the clearest denunciation of Movement poetics.

It begins by refusing the notion that it is an anthology of English poetry,[13] referencing the history of perceptions of English poetry since the 1950s and polemical anthologies that lay claim to pre-eminent achievement within the inclusive reference of national representation. Crozier and Longville refuse the exclusivity of fashion by a sectional view of change and difference so as not to be seen as covering the social divisions and otherness implicit in our national culture. They accused the Movement poets of employing a common rhetoric that foreclosed the possibilities of poetic language as well as the scope and character of poetic discourse in relation to the self, to knowledge, history and the world. Moreover, language was always to be grounded in the presence of a legitimating voice of an impersonally collective tone that was subsumed within a closed cultural programme.

They further lay claim to the Movement's wholesale rewriting of the history of modern poetry and the exclusion of parts of that history, the line from Pound and William Carlos Williams, and beyond to Olson, Oppen, Dorn and so forth,[14] this being a unifying connection between the contributors to the anthology, many of whom had also been *English Intelligencer* contributors.

The title of the anthology aptly summarises Crozier and Longville's ethos that poetry is an art in relation to language with various artifice and rules that apply to specific rather than to general occasions. Another unifying connection between the contributors that the editors cite was that many had established their own publishing houses and journals. I think, though, that there is an absence in their account and that is the impact of *The English Intelligencer*. It is the big connection. Firstly, it established the idea of exchange between interested individuals, often friends, although not exclusively, and a community of risk and possibility. The model for *The English Intelligencer* was the San Francisco journal, *Open Space*, initiated by Stan Persky in 1964 to provide a regular forum for a community of North Beach poets that included Robert Duncan, Jack Spicer, Robin Blaser and Joanne Kyger. The idea of *Open Space* had been to provide a context to the poetry and politics of the group and immediacy to the writing. Secondly, despite the difficulties of overcoming preconceived notions of publication, *The English Intelligencer* eventually became a communal forum of exchange, exploration and criticism that opened up new areas for many of its prominent contributors. As such, it underwrites the direction of many of its contributors and holds them a distinct relationship.

Crozier identified the period from 1956 to 1963 when critics, such as Donald Davie, Robert Conquest and Al Alvarez, moved the focus of attention away from the achievements and interests of the Forties poets to the Movement and confessional poets.[15] That shift can be said to start with the death of Dylan Thomas in 1953, and his literary executors, especially Kingsley Amis—who became a prominent Movement novelist and critic—doing much to detract from the achievement of Thomas and Forties poets generally.

The Forties had seen a great revival in poetic activity, as the archival work of A.T. Tolley[16] and others[17] has shown, and a growing interest in European and American poetics through Wrey Gardiner's Grey Walls Press, Tambimuttu's *Poetry London* and Poetry London Editions and John Lehmann's *Penguin New Writing*. It was a period, partly due to the Second World War, when the cultural exchange between London, Paris and New York was at a peak. Thus, the New York poet, Edward Field, was first published in Wrey Gardiner's *Poetry Quarterly* in London in 1946, and during his time as a fighter pilot in England he met many literary and artistic figures at the Gargoyle Club in Soho. Similarly, David Gascoyne, Rayner Heppenstall, W.S. Graham, Ruthven Todd, Norman Cameron, Nicholas Moore, Charles Madge, Kathleen Raine, Humphrey Jennings and Dylan Thomas, to name a few, all utilised London's Zwemmer's Bookshop for the latest artistic, literary and philosophical developments to arrive from Europe.

Crozier's interest in Forties poetry led him to contact J.F. Hendry, a survivor from that period and to write an introduction to his work in Iain Sinclair's anthology *Conductors of Chaos* (Picador 1996), a poetry anthology where other Forties poets were introduced, for example Nicholas Moore by Peter Riley, and given space. Crozier was instrumental in reviving interest in Hendry, the "New Apocalypse" and Forties poetry more generally, through his essay, 'Thrills and frills: poetry as figures of empirical lyricism' in *Society and Literature 1945*

Letter 15: Andrew Crozier

–1970, edited by Alan Sinfield (Methuen 1983).

I thought about connection in relation to Crozier because of his attention to context and historical placement. In my dealings with him, I found him to be modest and self-effacing. He effectively helped create a context, and thus a readership, for the *English Intelligencer*'s contributors, the poets whom he published with Ferry Press, and in *A Various Art*. He was clearly not prescriptive about any one approach or orthodoxy of intent and was at pains to point readers towards a diversity of achievement and fields of interest. In these more dogmatic times that is a salutary lesson.

Crozier's own poetry removed the lyrical self so as to enact a closer encounter with the particularity of things in the world. The poem, '(i.m. Rolf Dieter Brinkman)', was occasioned by the movement of ducklings around a pond and recalled a discussion about the volume of foliage on a summer branch 'which dips / toward the water to be reflected / in words that condense like the image // of each leaf shifting over the others while unreflected light flickers' and ends 'all language is truth / through a bed of dry leaves when evaporation / ceases and our words turn and fall / flickering with our life upon the earth.'[18]

Notes

[1] John Rodker, *Poems and Adolphe 1920* Ed. Andrew Crozier Manchester: Carcanet Press 1996
[2] Andrew Crozier introduces his selection from J.F. Hendry in *Conductors of Chaos* Ed. Ian Sinclair London: Picador 1996 pp. 72–73
[3] Crozier also edited Carl Rakosi, *Poems 1923–1941* Los Angeles: Sun and Moon Press 1995
[4] Peter Riley, *Tracks and Mineshafts* Matlock: Grosseteste Press 1983 p.23
[5] Ibid p.27
[6] See Peter Barry, *Poetry Wars: British Poetry of the 1970s and the Battle of Earls Court* Cambridge: Salt Publishing 2006
[7] Robert Conquest Ed., *New Lines–II* London: Macmillan 1963
[8] See Andrew Crozier, 'The World, The World: A Reading of John Riley's Poetry' in *For John Riley* edited by Tim Longville Wirksworth Grosseteste Press 1979 pp. 97–104
[9] See Ian Brinton, 'The Death of Andrew Crozier' *Eyewear* sourced at http://toddswift.blogspot.com/2008/04/death-of-andrew-crozier.html
[10] See Drew Milne, 'Agoraphobia, and the embarrassment of manifestos' *Jacket* 20 p. 11 sourced at http://jacketmagazine.com/20/pt-dm-agora.html
[11] Andrew Crozier & Tim Longville Eds, *A Various Art* Manchester: Carcanet Press 1987 pp.11–14
[12] Ibid p.14
[13] Ibid p.11
[14] Ibid p.12
[15] Andrew Crozier 'Thrills and frills: poetry as figures of empirical lyricism' in *Society And Literature 1945–1970* Ed. Alan Sinfield London: Methuen 1983 pp. 199–233
[16] A. T. Tolley, *The Poetry of the Forties* Manchester: Manchester University Press 1985
[17] Andrew Sinclair, *War Like A Wasp: The Lost Decade of the Forties* London: Hamish Hamilton 1989
[18] *A Various Art* p.82

Letter 16: John Riley

In my last talk I mentioned that Andrew Crozier shared some affinities with the poet, John Riley, an early contributor to *The English Intelligencer*. This is particularly noticeable in Crozier's poem, 'The Veil Poem',[1] where he employs a probing lyrical self to see beneath cognitive perception to unveil the shifts of light and dark. Moreover, Crozier repeatedly refers to light, mirrors, windows and glass in his poetry to indicate a concern with the processes of perception. Thus in the first stanza of 'Light In The Air' we read "Light floods the retina / then vanishes along the / optic nerve to reappear / as what we see"[2] and in 'The Veil Poem', Crozier seems to be concerned with probing and enacting the processes by which the self articulates the shifts not only between the shades of light and dark, waking and sleeping but also between partial and impartial knowledge. The poem effectively shows how the self is "drawn" as vessel and vehicle, hemmed and pressed in by a wall of both light, darkness and disputed colour. There are echoes of Coleridge's 'Frost at Midnight', John Dee in its reference to "the repeated tracery of magic in / cardinal numbers", John Donne in its metaphysics of incompleteness and John Riley in his probing of how to respond to light and the world. Although Riley might well have wished to move beyond the concept of "the hermetic / correspondence of forms hidden beneath appearance"[3] into a more commonplace understanding.

I would like to contextualise John Riley's poetry and give some idea of its range and integrity. Far from Blake Morrison and Andrew Motion's contemptuous assertion in the *Penguin Book of Contemporary British Poetry* that "very little seemed to be happening"[4] in the Sixties, the scope of Riley's work and that of other *English Intelligencer* contributors would indicate otherwise. When I first encountered Riley's poetry in the mid-Seventies in the various pamphlets and poetry magazines that I found in Compendium Bookshop, it was like a revelation to find an English poet that was speaking in the present and yet out of time and in the visionary tradition. This was a poet quite distinct from the official poets and seemingly in touch with a wider European humanism that allowed for difference and the idea of a melting pot and also with post-Poundian American poetry.

John Riley (1937–1978) was born and went to school in Leeds, Yorkshire. After National Service in the Royal Air Force, which he spent in Germany and during which time he learned Russian, he read English at Pembroke College, Cambridge from 1958 to 1961. He was thus an exact contemporary of Tim Longville and the satirist, Peter Cook, also studying English at Pembroke, and a near contemporary of J.H. Prynne and R.F. Langley who studied English at Jesus College. Bill Oddie, who followed Cook into writing and performing radio comedy, began studying English at Pembroke College in Riley's final year. Cook was a precocious undergraduate figure at Pembroke, creating a legend even greater than that of Ted Hughes in the early Fifties. Whereas Cook left Pembroke for Soho, Riley worked in various schools around Cambridge after graduating, and became acquainted with other Cambridge-based poets. In 1966 he took up a teaching post at Bicester, near Oxford. It was during this period that Andrew Crozier invited him to contribute to *The English Intelligencer* and he began to write his distinctive poems. He founded the Grosseteste Press and *Grosseteste Review* with Tim Longville, and published his first book, *Ancient and Modern* in 1967. Here in its title we have possible notions that the author advocates both the old and new or that the new comes out of the old and are mutually held together. Riley's poetry is precise and attentive to detail. It has a tremendous clarity and that probably stems from an admiration for the techniques of George Oppen, Charles Olson, to whom he wrote a memorial poem 'in memoriam Charles Olson' (*The Collected Works* Grosseteste 1980 p. 147) and Robert Creeley. Its broken exactness owes something to Creeley's early sixties love poems. Thus in the poem, 'January 1966', we read: "if there's time / I'll plant a tree // there where that blackbird is, a / sycamore / for speed // against the black wall".[5]

Beneath the admiration for Oppen, Olson and Creeley, one might detect a background in Pound studies. Indeed his press was named after the Neo-Platonist theologian and philosopher, Robert Grosseteste (c1170–1253), who inspired Pound. Grosseteste argued that light was the first corporeal form and that light was the basis of all matter. Love and truth were reached through illumination by divine grace. From studying thirteenth-century Neo-Platonists, including Grosseteste, Pound derived the idea of light, the radiant world, the self-interfering patterns from which and through which all corporeality flows and this impacted upon his poetry in the *Cantos*. He wrote in an essay on Guido Calvacanti about the significance of light and the loss of the radiant world "where one thought cuts through another with a clean edge, a world of moving energies" ... a world of "magnetisms that take form, that are seen, or that border the visible, the matter of Dante's *paradiso*, the glass under water, the form that sees a form in the mirror ..."[6] According to Donald Davie in *Ezra Pound: Poet as Sculptor*,

Letter 16: John Riley

which compared Pound's use of language to a sculptor's use of stone, the constituents of the *Cantos* are components arranged in space. It is a poetry, Davie writes, "that characteristically moves forward only hesitantly, gropingly, and slowly; which often seems to float across the page as much as it moves down it; in which, if the perceptions are cast in the form of sentences, the sentence is bracketed off and, as it were, folded in on itself so as to seem equal with a disjointed phrase; a poetry (we might almost say) of the noun rather than the verb."[7] This is a useful description of the technique of Pound, Olson and Creeley and one that Riley doubtless would have known through his contact with Davie and others at Cambridge.

Riley's poetry has that slow movement and lucidity and that same floating across the page as well as something different, as in 'The World Itself, The Long Poem Foundered' with lines such as "A daisy grows. A girl passes. A girl passes along / The wet night street, the houses opposite are luminous" and later probing with, "How to trace longing beyond sight, / Removed beyond sensible reaching? And to give it voice?"[8]

Here the first person narrator is characteristically looking out of a window and probing with a calm restlessness. It is a knowing inner voice that is caught at the edge of his knowledge and relationships and love. Note the large gaps between some of the parts of the poem and its title indicating a compression or rejection from a long poem. The 'Long Poem Foundered' could for example be a rejection of Pound, as the modern founder of the long poem and that would entail the rejection of the institution around Poundian aesthetics. It could equally indicate a broken and abandoned longer poem of which 'The World Itself' resembles and is the equivalent of. The idea of the world as broken and abandoned in poetry and elsewhere might give the first person narrator some edge. This poem indicates Riley's constant probing of how "to trace longing beyond sight / Removed beyond sensible reaching? And to give it voice?" Birds, emissaries of the spiritual, are also to be traced "round-eyed". A restless, searching intelligence informs every line as well as a successive movement of stillness that serves to suspend each image and verbal event in a continuous present. Riley's poetry characteristically has a calm restlessness in which the calm and restlessness, the lyric and counter lyric, are held in balanced conflict and repetition. It is this ability to hold both the balance and conflict and repetition together with fresh language that distinguishes Riley's work. Note the repetition of key words, such as, "A girl", "love", "longing", "full", "voice", "trace", "birds", "beauty", "world", "light", "moon", "hair" "eyes", "face", "time" and "rain". The third part of the poem consists of a full repetition of key words, such as "birds", "beauty", "longing", "voice" and "love" and serves to re-set the poem's theme in the fourth line, "Your voice, moving me to a celebration of it, love". A line that refuses any easy closure as it holds the possibility of "voice" and "love" both being subject and object in both cases. Several of these key words occur in repetition in many other poems. He was drawn by the "ancient" certainties of ritual repetition, as John Hall has written,[9] where ritual itself is a set of repetitions and a way of ending without ending. Many of his concerns are encapsulated in the fourth part of the poem:

> A stillness encompassing movement
> With enormous beauty still to answer to.
>
> Blackness seeps through the closed door, douses the lamp.
> It is a longing for the same world, and a different world. [10]

The seemingly contradictory statements of the first and fourth lines serve to enact their own contradictions as fixtures of the world by a perceiving self that seeks both the certainties of the past and transformation of the present world.

In 1970 Riley gave up primary school teaching in order to spend more time writing and editing. He moved in the winter of 1970–71 briefly to Fowey in Cornwall, which provided the stimulus for a number of poems, such as 'Rough Tor, Cornwall, this landscape what song', and then returned to Leeds, where he lived for the rest of his life. He married Carol Brown in 1973. He became absorbed in French, German and Russian poetry, translating Hölderlin, Pasternak and Mandelstam. This reinforced his disposition to view the world in religious terms and in 1977 he joined the Russian Orthodox Church. He was mugged to death in uncertain circumstances on the night of 27/28 October 1978. A memorial volume, *For John Riley* edited by Tim Longville appeared in 1979. Tim Longville edited *The Collected Works* (Grosseteste) in 1980 and Riley's work was included in Andrew

Letter 16: John Riley

Crozier and Tim Longville's *A Various Art* anthology (Carcanet 1987) and Keith Tuma's landmark *Anthology of Twentieth Century British and Irish Poetry* (Oxford University Press USA 2001). Tuma selected the long poem, 'Czargrad' to illustrate Riley's concern with the Orthodox Church and post-Poundian poetics. A *Selected Poems* (Carcanet) edited by Michael Grant appeared in 1995.

Riley's poems characteristically look out, from a window, to probe what is known of the world. They typically proceed through an accumulation of statements about the phenomenal world with all its pain, longing and loss and end in an unsettling doubt where the song is undone. I take the perceiving narrator in Riley's poetry, following Andrew Crozier,[11] to be transfigured by love and concerned with placement. The narrator is absorbed within a metaphysical world of linkages that are set up in the poems as binaries and opposites. Thus the domestic is linked to the divine, One is linked to All, and here and now to everywhere. There are no spiritual discoveries or epiphanies but rather there is a journey into the world, the planet and eternity, from certainty to an unsettling doubt. This journey is in the continual present and takes the form of an intense response to light, love and the world and is re-enacted with each new day and poem. After re-reading his poems, one is struck by the realisation that Riley is one of the greatest philosophers of love and incompleteness since John Donne.

Poem after poem in Riley's work seems to sing and yet deny the possibility of song. Each lyric contains its own counter lyric and an evasion of easy closure. Thus in 'Love Poem' (*The Collected Works* p. 66) we read: "Not that anything has to be improved. / Simply that everything must be done away with." This impulse to undercut the lyrical voice with an opposing one is also seen in the poem, 'Second Fragment', from the start: "I put out the light and listen to the rain / Example taken from history—she loved"

> The rain: but that won't do for she loves it still
> And perhaps awake as I she lies at home
>
> And listens to the rain that once beat on Rome
> Or fell gently on the Galilean hills

Note the beginning of the second line undercutting the attempt to elegise and the correction in the third line "The rain: but that won't do for she loves it still" and then the recourse to placement within the history of Empire and Christianity. The poem continues: "This time of year is so beautiful / One can almost abandon oneself to it".

This attempt to eulogise is again interrupted, cut up and counter pointed to the point of anguish culminating in the final three couplets and piercingly so in the penultimate: "We renew ourselves completely how often— / Daily we slit dumb throats and watch the blood run".[12]

Internally, then, this poem has a number of continuous struggles between the "I" and the "One", the "still" and the "rain", the "fell gently" and the "slit dumb throats", the "indifference" and "believers", the "light" being put out in the present and in the past, and so on.

Riley's second book, *What Reason Was* (Grosseteste 1970) is linked by the progress and breakdown of a relationship and the longing for a permanence that is beyond reach. It is marked by loss and absence and hope against fear, through eternity or the eternal return. This is perhaps seen best in 'Poem on These Poems',[13] a commentary on earlier poems, a technique subsequently employed by Bill Griffiths,[14] with its "Myrtle tree of heaven, white-scented flowers / Of Venus" that "Will kill me for ever and ever." The poem beautifully sketches out the origin and arc of his poetic concerns, seen both as a "voice" and "voiceless eye" and thus isolating the imbalance between speech acts and perception over time. Here Riley as ever holds the tensions of binaries and opposites in balance and the loss and absence inherent in love and light, again leads to brutal anguish, as in the second stanza's: "My God my love I cannot see or sing, / There is no part left of me that does not hurt". This reinforces the idea that love and light both blind. If Riley's world is constantly threatened by loss and absence, the longing to sing out that is curtailed by an unsettling doubt, this poem finally finds a placement beyond the usual binaries that frame and limit the probing self. The ending gives two placements for the narrator and reader, one in the 'voiceless eye' of the poem and the second "at the foot of the tree" of knowledge.

Letter 16: John Riley

Notes

[1] Andrew Crozier, 'The Veil Poem' in Andrew Crozier & Tim Longville Eds, *A Various Art* Manchester: Carcanet Press 1987 pp.71–76
[2] Ibid p.83
[3] Ibid p.73
[4] Blake Morrison & Andrew Motion, *Penguin Book of Contemporary British Poetry* London: Penguin 1982 p.11
[5] John Riley, *The Collected Works* Ed. Tim Longville Wirksworth: Grosseteste Press 1980 p.43
[6] Hugh Kenner, *The Pound Era* London: Pimlico 1991 p. 451
[7] Donald Davie, *Ezra Pound: Poet as Sculptor* London: Routledge Kegan Paul 1965. Davie also comments upon Adrian Stokes and Pound's *Cantos* in this book.
[8] John Riley, *The Collected Works* pp. 103–105
[9] John Hall, 'John Riley, poet' *Tears in the Fence* 20, Spring 1998 p.63
[10] John Riley, *The Collected Works* p.104
[11] Andrew Crozier, 'The World, The World: A Reading of John Riley's Poetry' in *For John Riley* Grosseteste 1979 pp. 97–104
[12] John Riley, *The Collected Works* p.62
[13] Ibid p.126
[14] Bill Griffiths, *Collected Earlier Poems (1966–80)* Eds. Alan Halsey and Ken Edwards, Hastings: Reality Street 2010 p. 266

Letter 17: David Gascoyne

Poetic fashions ebb and flow and there are always marginalised figures who pursue fields of interest that are on the edge of acceptability. The boundaries of poetic discourse are always blurred and being challenged by successive avant-gardes. The poetic field itself is infinitely expansive, rather than limited to easily identifiable categories, due to the nature of language and to the bohemian inclination towards difference and "the other". If we remove this from our analysis we have a less than dynamic vision of poetic discourse and endeavour and fail to see the myriad ways in which poets have produced sound and written texts, have questioned how to use language, form and the lyrical voice. In short, we fail to see that there is a vast history of alternative poetries. For most of the last century, these poetries have been concerned with the interface between the public and private, between the self, experience and language in place and time and how to produce a radical poetics. These poetries can be seen as counter to the Movement and its successors, and their continued anti-modernism and anti-internationalism which, in the words of Andrew Crozier and Tim Longville, "foreclosed the possibilities of poetic language within its own devices."[1] Overall, and underlying this, there has also been a continuous dispute about what constitutes the central tradition of English poetry.

The impact of this cultural nationalism has been such that many Forties poets have been attacked and forgotten. Their history of outward-looking and international engagement has been marginalised and downgraded by Movement and post-Movement critics. This is seen most clearly in the exclusion of Dylan Thomas, W.S. Graham, Norman Cameron, Lynn Roberts, Ruthven Todd, Nicholas Moore, George Barker, Humphrey Jennings, Philip O'Connor, Kathleen Raine, George Reavey, Sean Rafferty, Wrey Gardiner, Tambimuttu, J.F. Hendry, Burns Singer, Henry Treece, Hamish Henderson, Ruth Pitter, Vernon Watkins and their friends and associates.

The situation of one Forties poet was such that, in April 1974, he found himself listening to a woman read the poem 'September Sun: 1947' to a group of mental patients on the Isle of Wight. A tall, sad-looking man in a group of severely depressed inmates finally convinced Judy Lewis that he indeed was the poet, David Gascoyne, who had written the poem. Here we are in the midst of a hole in Gascoyne's life. This is the man who had been a massive presence and key figure in the late Thirties and Forties in English and French culture, mixing and arguing within Marxism, psychoanalysis, Catholic mysticism, alchemy and Surrealism. This is the man who, in 1964, had been arrested at the Élysée Palace on his way to warn President de Gaulle of a forthcoming apocalypse and whose previous twenty years of life were still cast in shadow, seemingly lost, albeit highlighted by his December 1955 radio meditation, 'Night Thoughts' and the publication of his *Collected Poems* in 1965.

He had been a precocious figure. He had published his first poetry volume, *Roman Balcony* (1932) aged 16, in the vein of Rilke, first novel, *Opening Day*, aged 17, written *A Short Survey of Surrealism* (1935), aged 19, and helped organise the 1936 International Surrealist Exhibition at Burlington House in London. His immediate circle was a distinct mixture of neo-Romantic poets that frequented the bookshops and pubs of Fitzrovia: Dylan Thomas, George Barker, Ruthven Todd, Roger Roughton and Norman Cameron, and recent Cambridge graduates, Humphrey Jennings, Roland Penrose, Charles Madge and Kathleen Raine. He had spent 1933 in Paris, having been drawn by the avant-garde magazines he found in Zwemmer's bookshop in London's Charing Cross Road. He was soon at the centre of the Surrealist movement in Paris with André Breton, Max Ernst and so on. From his *Collected Journals 1936–1942* we find Gascoyne in London and Paris, advocating a revolutionary literature that is not didactic or social-realist, and striving to move into a deeper literary area than that occupied by the Auden generation. In Paris he absorbs himself in European poetry and philosophy and writes *Hölderlin's Madness* (1938), inspired by the translations of Jean Pierre Jouve, and sees the need for a great spiritual reawakening and rebirth to be part of any political revolution. Writing at a time of international danger, he turned to the Book of Revelation and the concept of the artist as a prophet.[2] In the same period that he wrote *Poems 1937–1942* (Poetry London Editions 1943), illustrated by Graham Sutherland, and was translating Breton, Eluard, Dali and so on for Roughton's *Contemporary Poetry & Prose* magazine, he interestingly compares his European conception of poetry with the Auden Generation's poetry of rhetoric and argument. For him poetry is, in essence, a journey of discovery to the void and beyond and operates on a deeper level than that of statement or reportage.

Letter 17: David Gascoyne

To those who want to limit the horizon of English poetry, Gascoyne is simply brushed aside as a figure caught up in obscure French poetry and Surrealism, neatly forgetting that he was a distinctly English poet, working as much in the English visionary tradition as that of European poetry and philosophy. The arc of his poetic development is distinctly international and draws upon a wide range of sources. It stems from a period of rich intellectual exchange in Paris and London that provided the context to his poetry. I would like to say a few words about that context and offer some introductory notes to some of his poems.

Gascoyne's *Poems 1937–1942* marks a movement away from his earlier Surrealist work, *Man's Life Is This Meat* (1936), which established him as the leading surrealist poet in England. Published by Tambimuttu, a Sri Lankan poet and publisher of *Poetry London* and PL Editions, it includes a cover and several edgy and alarming black and red ink-drawings by the painter, Graham Sutherland, which augment and add to the effect of the whole. Sutherland had exhibited at the 1936 Surrealist exhibition; here, his work seems to be echoing Gascoyne's journey towards revelation.

The book is full of dedications and notations to the bohemian culture of Paris and London. The most dominant word in the book is "sky". There are translations of Jouve, elegies for Wolf Berthold and Roger Roughton, a poem to Benjamin Fondane, as well as a whole section in French dedicated to the memory of the composer, Alban Berg. A range of traditional and modernist forms and styles are employed, which serve to upset any natural flow to the book.

Gascoyne's over-riding intellectual concern was to unite the subjective and the objective, the personal and the political, surrealism and political commitment. He strived to formulate what he called "dialectical supermaterialism", a reconciliation of metaphysics with revolutionary ideology. His poetic sources and inspirations are a distinct amalgam of the visionary landscapes of neo-Romantic poetry and painting, such as his mentor, the editor of *New Verse*, Geoffrey Grigson's enthusiasm for Samuel Palmer and the landscape of southern England, the surrealists reading of Freud, such as Salvador Dalí's theory of paranoia which inspired Jacques Lacan's development of the concept of the Imaginary and Jean-Pierre Jouve's work on sublimation, which connected Freud with Christianity, and mixing of the mystical and the erotic in his quest to move beyond the void. Gascoyne was actively reading the latest philosophical and psychoanalytical essays, absorbing Heidegger and early existentialist writings, translating a wide range of new essays and poetry by Dalí, Breton, Eluard and Jouve that was tackling ontological questions. All this was fuelled by a growing amphetamine addiction at a time of uncertainty over his sexuality. He later confided that these were the two major omissions from his *Journals*.[3] He was actively talking about these matters in the cafés and bars of Montmartre and undergoing psychoanalysis with Jouve's wife, Blanche Reverchon, which proved unhelpful. All these sources were instrumental in leading Gascoyne to a more visionary, religious poetry. Jouve, in particular, had written that the only answer to the void of time was to find in the poetic act a religious perspective.[4]

I would like to briefly look at two of Gascoyne's poems, 'Ecce Homo' and 'The Gravel-pit Field', from *Poems 1937–1942*.

'Ecce Homo'[5] is often quoted as the poem that led to Gascoyne's ostracism from official Surrealism for its reference to "Christ of Revolution and of Poetry" in stanzas 10–12. Gascoyne's Christ, though, as Kathleen Raine has noted, is like Blake's, the "divine humanity" in all humankind, the spirit of imagination and of prophecy.[6] The key reference to the "eternal Christ" is in stanza 2 line "He is in agony till the world's end". The poem turns upon a mystical response to international fascism that places the current international violence in the context of larger and more enduring suffering, "the slow / Torture of God" "in agony till the world's end". The "black shirts" of Italian and Spanish fascism along with the "raised armed salutes" of the Nazis are referenced in stanza 4, lines 3 and 4.

Gascoyne at this time was also deepening his reading within the European alchemical tradition. He had known the work of Emmanuel Swedenborg since he was a schoolboy at Salisbury Cathedral School and had progressed through the German alchemical tradition from Cornelius Agrippa's *Occult Philosophy* (1650) to Novalis' *Hymns to the Night* (1800). The concept of the eternal is certainly derived from his reading of Boehme and Novalis, and his reading background in Blake. In his *Journal* entry on 23 April 1939, we find Gascoyne in the midst of spiritual experience and writing: "The essential nature of the experience being Negation. The void, das Nichts, Nada, le Néant. Practically the only image that presents itself at all strongly to me is a black vacuum in (or through) which two eyes are fixedly staring" and searching for the right tone to write poems about man's present spiritual crisis. [7] In 'Ecce Homo' he calls upon the "Christ of Revolution and of Poetry" to "Redeem our sterile misery" so that "Man's long journey through the night / May not have been in vain". The 'Miserere' section of *Poems* sketches a "revelation of despair", the contemporary spiritual condition, and shows a divine presence in moments of lucid subjectivity. This subjectivity returns the world to an authentic objectivity. It is suffering and a journey to the edge of the void that allows this transitory illumination of the divine presence or god of imagination. The void, here, being the result of the negation of the divine presence. This worldview is a distinct mixture of alchemical, surrealistic and ontological thinking stemming from the cafés and bars of Paris' Left Bank inscribed within an English visionary landscape, as in poems such as 'The Gravel-pit Field'.[8]

The arc of 'The Gravel-pit Field' is from the ordinary objective to the extraordinary subjective with the bleak light of the March evening becoming the light of transformation. Here the imagination takes hold of the real as a succession of image objects is transformed. The snail shells become rare stones and the mongrel bones become relics of some saint, the writing on the woodbine cigarette packet becomes the writing on the wall from Daniel 5:25 and so on. This culminates in the gravel-pit field's "apotheosis" becoming a "No man's land" and "tabernacle" enabling a communion "between this world and the beyond". The transformation of image objects is surely alchemical. The poem was written at a time when Gascoyne and other surrealists, such as Breton and Ernst, were drawing upon alchemical sources and inspiration. The use of a gravel-pit is significant in that it is unconsecrated ground and the site of late eighteenth century dissenting meetings, such as held by Dr. Joseph Priestley on 19 April 1793 to preach on Psalm 46 line one "God is our refuge and strength, a very present help in trouble" and on 28 February 1794 and other fast days.[9] Priestley was also a Francophile, believer in revelation and prophecy and writing at a time when England was at war. The use of "No man's land" reminds us of that area between two warring forces which is held by neither and where both sides are

Letter 17: David Gascoyne

free to go as well as an area of land that is not owned by any particular individual or agency and tabernacle being a place of worship by nonconformists as well as a receptacle for the Eucharist and a fixed or movable habitation.

Gascoyne's poems stem from the creative centre of Europe. His concern is essentially with the boundaries and thresholds of consciousness, stemming from the discoveries of Freud, the surrealists, through the early existentialist movement, which Gascoyne splits into two separate groupings and sharply differentiates his perspective from that of Sartre's, to Heidegger's thinking on authenticity, being and time, to the frontiers of madness in Hölderlin and his novelist friend, Antonia White, and contemporary occult and magical practice.

It is in the darkness of the last century that he set about trying to find some light, went mad, and recovered to re-read his past.

After Judy Lewis rescued Gascoyne, they married and he became part of the poetry-reading circuit, reading to packed audiences at Cambridge and at the Sorbonne, and he was later honoured by the French Government. His radio poem, 'Night Thoughts', with its pre-Situationist mapping of the deserted city, had an impact on writers and poets such as Iain Sinclair, Jeremy Reed and Aidan Andrew Dun. Reed provided the introduction to Gascoyne's poems in the *Conductors of Chaos* anthology (Picador 1996), edited by Iain Sinclair, noting Gascoyne's "total commitment" to his art and compassion for the outsider who lives by "inner rather than social dictates".[10]

The situation is changing slowly. The Forties is increasingly seen as a watershed decade and more critical attention is being given to its neglected poets. Robert Fraser, who wrote a critical biography of George Barker,[11] is now writing a biography of David Gascoyne and Rod Mengham is also working on a Gascoyne study. Enitharmon Press have recently published *Despair Has Wings: Selected Poems by Jean Pierre Jouve Translated by David Gascoyne* along with various letters and other materials. More discoveries on Gascoyne's extraordinary life and previously lost or unpublished material are also forthcoming. There is also now plenty of critical attention being given to W.S. Graham. There was a recent symposium of essays on Seán Rafferty at *Intercapillary Space* edited by Alistair Noon;[12] Andrew Duncan's recent book *Origins of the*

Underground (Salt 2008) has chapters on Gascoyne and other Forties poets, and Peter Riley has an essay on Dylan Thomas forthcoming in *Poetry Wales*.

Notes

[1] Andrew Crozier & Tim Longville Eds, *A Various Art* Manchester: Carcanet Press 1987 p. 2
[2] David Gascoyne, *Collected Journals 1936–1942* London: Skoob Books 1991 pp. 169–170, 178–179, 255–257, 263, 274
[3] Ibid pp. 336–402
[4] A.T. Tolley, *The Poetry of the Forties in Britain* Manchester: Manchester University Press 1985 pp.141–148
[5] David Gascoyne, *Poems 1937–1942* London: PL Editions / Nicholson & Watson 1943 p.5
[6] Kathleen Raine, 'Introduction' in David Gascoyne: *Selected Prose 1934–1996* London: Enitharmon Press 1998 p.18
[7] David Gascoyne, *Collected Journals* p.256
[8] David Gascoyne, *Poems 1937–42* pp.59–60
[9] Dr. Joesph Priestley, A Sermon Preached at The Gravel Pit Meeting, In Hackney April 19th 1793 sourced at http://www.archive.org/stream/asermonpreached00priegoog
[10] Jeremy Reed introduces his selection from David Gascoyne in *Conductors of Chaos* Iain Sinclair Ed. London: Picador 1996 p. 372
[11] Robert Fraser, T*he Chameleon Poet: A Life of George Barker* London: Jonathan Cape 2001
[12] See http://intercapillaryspace.blogspot.com/2008/02/sean-rafferty-symposium.html

Letter 18: Forests

My first recollection of entering Piddles Wood near Fiddleford in the mid-Sixties is of sinking into wet mud along the rutted uphill path and of the constant patter of raindrops on a dense flora of shrubs, ferns, creepers and moss. Enchanted by this ancient woodland of oak, ash and hazel, I became a regular visitor and soon discovered the remains of a campfire strewn with cider and methylated-spirit bottles and a makeshift stove. A little higher uphill was the disused brick house that had been the home of a woodman in the Fifties and an orchard of apple and plum trees. The place seemed alive with living things and yet had an otherworldly nature due to the variation and nature of sounds and the prospect of encountering some stag, tramp or creature. I became aware of the way cuckoos and owls mimic human voices and of the extraordinary variety of butterflies and moths. This early experience of ancient woodland eventually led to poems and an interest in woods in social and literary history as well as what is now called biodiversity and ecology. Unlike my father and grandfather, I am not a carpenter although I do follow the happenings around my local woods and that filters into my poems.

Whenever I walk Piddles Wood now, I recall the Dorset Elizabethan poet, George Turbeville's *Noble Art of Venerie or Hunting* (1576).[1] Turbeville (1540–1610) was from nearby Winterborne Whitchurch and belonged to the old Dorset family recalled by Thomas Hardy in his novel, *Tess of the d'Ubervilles* (1888). His book is a manual on the etiquette and language of all things connected to hunting. It is also a poetry book with a commendatory poem on the noble art by George Gascoigne, the Green Knight, and poems by Turbeville from the viewpoint of the huntsman and the various hunted animals. The book, dedicated to the Queen's Master of Hart Hounds, is a work of translation from English, French, Latin, Italian and Dutch sources designed to offer the best guide to noble and gentlemen available and it became an immensely popular and important work in shaping hunting behaviour for the several centuries. The virtues, nature and properties of stags, hounds and dogs are identified and the deer hunter is taught how to read behaviour and physical signs in animals. The book also features one of the first appearances in English of Reynard the Fox, the ballad popularised by John Masefield in his 1919 poem and a staple of BBC radio broadcasting during the twentieth century. Based on mainly anonymous late twelfth- and thirteenth-century French poets, Turbeville omits the bawdy and comic elements of the original. It is his book on hunting, far more than his *Epitaphes, Epigrams, Songs and Sonnets* (1567) and translations of Ovid, that give him importance in English social and literary history. For his guidebook and poems have their opposite in illegal hunting, or poaching, and in the history of those excluded from the noble art that sought access to the bounty of the wood. Poaching continues in 2008 and is a business for some and a form of economic survival for others. Increasingly well-organised at the top end of the business are those that organise stag hunts in Piddles Wood at £1,000 per gun, and at the bottom end are joy-hunters who lack the income to do much more, and people stealing kindling wood and timber. In between are warring factions of gypsies and gamekeepers that roam far and wide in acts of poaching and cruelty.

Hunting forests were subject to harsh Forest Law, imposed by the Normans, with punishments of castration and mutilation. Indeed, the word "forest" was originally a judicial term meaning land that had been placed off limits by royal decree. By the twelfth century there were 66 Royal Forests and 70 private chases controlled by strict Forest Law. Here the King and other nobles had the right to keep deer, wild boar and other prey. "Forest" also carries within it a meaning of being outside the public domain and it is this meaning that poets have utilised. Forests and woods, then, are potentially where the world is turned upside down, as in Shakespeare's *As You Like It* or *A Midsummer Night's Dream*. It is a place of sexual discovery and assignation, danger and deceit, where pagan spirits can take over a man, such as Falstaff, as in *The Merry Wives of Windsor*. Things can be different and the pastoral can be disrupted to allow otherness to enter. Protest poems against Forest law date back to the Old English poem, 'The Rhyme of William' found in the *Peterborough Chronicle* (1087).[2]

I would like to look at some forests as they appear in English poetry. This is a vast theme and I only intend these remarks as introductory and to dovetail into previous talks. From the seventeenth century the history of forests is one of progressive deforestation with attendant struggles over rights, access and poaching. Forest officers according to Forest Law that had been encoded since the twelfth century essentially kept royal forests fertile. As more land was turned over from the monarchy into chases and parks and eventual enclosure, the more non-landowners lost pasture, common rights and forest access.

Letter 16: Forests

Forest land became stripped of wood, turf, gorse and timber as private owners unwilling to compensate commoners with rights of pasture, turf and wood took advantage of their new market freedom. New money and new types of landowners produced barren and disputed forests. This divide between public men with landed property and the new private competitive men unmotivated by public spirit is seen in Alexander Pope's poem, 'Windsor Forest' (1713). Here Windsor Forest signifies an older order of values, land and custom, domestic peace and harmony, as in line 42 'And peace and plenty tell, a STUART reigns.' The poem celebrates a brief period of harmony between forest officials and foresters during Queen Anne's reign. The Forest, continually shrinking in size throughout the eighteenth century, was divided into parkland owned by the Crown and private owners, enclosed arable and meadow land, thick coppices and smaller woods, moor land and marginal lands with squatters. It was still highly regulated and from 1716 the harmony was destroyed by new forest laws brought in by the Whig government, leading to intense hostilities between poachers and forest officials between 1720 and 1723.[3] Pope, whose experience of growing up at Binfield on the western part of the forest underlay much of his pastoral poetry, celebrates the harmony of the forest economy with its balance between hunters and farmers. This is contrasted with the earlier tyranny of William III's reign, a tyranny which returned as Walpole's Government sided with the new moneyed interests against the foresters and passed the *Black Act* (1723), introducing the death penalty for breaking forest laws.

Eric Mottram's *Windsor Forest* (Pig Press 1979) draws upon the legend of Herne the Hunter first mentioned in *The Merry Wives of Windsor* and explores the historical and mythological origin of a specific wood demon. The poem serves as a local study of power relations within the forest over time and of a self in conflict with authority. It employs an open-field approach with a kind of Victorian sub-horror imagery derived from W. Harrison Ainsworth's historical romance, *Windsor Castle* (1844) and George Cruikshank's illustrations, supported by references to British and Celtic deities and reminders that the legend is based in part, at least, upon historical relations and conditions from the fourteenth century onwards. The lines are heavily compacted with information and references to how belief in a wood demon is ingrained in English culture and linked to widespread popular beliefs. The forester / narrator is tested, as in the legend, by the offer of liberation into demonic power and example of Herne, which he tries to resist, "I may be in league with darkness / but I have no wish to aid him" for his crimes.[4] This implicit association between Herne and darkness recalls the Windsor Forest poachers blacking their faces to disguise their identity in their struggle with forest officials as sketched by E.P. Thompson in *Whigs and Hunters*. The wood demon is the product of repression and revenge. "I have known no human passion except hatred and revenge." The poem ends with the forester seeing demonic energy "more through deeds" and "hunt horns" calling "the allegiances",[5] which implies a dual demonic nature in both sides of the divide. The poem catches the slippery nature and energy of a wood demon through sudden narrative shifts, and dense, arcane language which produces an unsettling effect. There is uncertainty over the range of possible meanings and inferences and their exact relationship to the narrative that requires further enquiry. For example, Herne is introduced as "wild spectral humanity" and described with "deer skins around tawny gaunt limbs" ... "a skull helmet antlered" / "phosphoric fire cut in links / rusted from his left arm chain / on his right wrist a horned owl / dilated taloned erect".[6]

This appears to be a description of Cruikshank's Herne illustrations. However, Mottram has added "phosphoric fire", "red balled" and "full cauldrons". The "phosphoric fire" could be a reference to Lucifer's fall making the connection with the fallen Herne and also introducing some notion of transformation from hunter to spirit to Satan or another demonised figure. Note the use of "inks" indicating relations beyond the links on chain-mail to preface this line of connection.

Windsor Forest is a complex poem that opens up a wide area of association. For example, it connects the dangers of the forest with forbidden and erotic love through the presence and quotation from Anne Boleyn's lover, Sir Thomas Wyatt, who presumably employed Herne to regain Anne and "now follows druid fire". Wyatt's sonnet "Whoso list to hunt", perhaps about Anne, acknowledges that he may hunt "an hind" no more. Herne's woodcraft is associated with Celtic deities and regeneration "on occasion he appeared as a monk in dark second skin", Actaeon, the Greek hunter who changed into a stag, and

Letter 16: Forests

Ogham script, the "three strikes" used to name a tree. Gypsies, amongst those squatting on the forest's margins, are also linked with Herne, through "skin" in a passage where the hunter and trapped buck appear to find release. Mottram developed his Herne investigations into *A Book of Herne*,[7] linking with Herne with the Green Man and widening his theme of a self in conflict with authority, desire and madness.

The Easter stag hunt that the poet John Clare witnessed in Epping Forest, north-east of Greater London in 1841, was an annual event from 1226 until 1858. He was affected that Easter Monday by standing next to "a stout, tall, young woman, dressed in a darkish fox-red, cotton gown as a milkmaid or farm-servant." He was a poet that to use Merleau-Ponty's phrase breathes "authentic speech".[8] He is awake to the nuances of each living being in Epping Forest and they invest his poetry with clarity as he names and speaks for them. Clare's poem "London versus Epping Forest" has become a powerful statement for the green movement in that it calls for responsible stewardship of the forest and its inhabitants. The narrator sees "London, like a shrub among the hills," ... "hid and lower than the bushes here" and "could not bear to see the tearing plough / Root up and steal the Forest from the poor, / But leave to freedom all she loves untamed, / The forest walk enjoyed and loved by all."[9]

The forest's greatness over London, that is a representation of commercial capital, is defined in terms of its measurement and ability to bestow freedom to all that exists within itself. This includes the poor whose freedoms are being eroded by the loss of forest land. Clare asserts the right to roam and access to wood's bounty for the poor at a time when enclosure reduced the Forest in size from 9,000 acres in 1793 to 7,000 acres in 1848.[10] His earlier poem 'To a Fallen Elm' proclaims the right to life for every living thing and by using an old tree evokes the full panoply of ancient statutes that won and protected the access and other rights denied by enclosure, saying "right was wrong and wrong was right". Clare's poem is quite distinct and more powerful than for example William Cowper's acquiescence to loss in 'The Poplar-field' (1784) or Gerard Manley Hopkins' lament for the loss of the Binsey poplars in 1879. For him the elm tree is as much a temporal as a spatial landmark and when a tree goes he is disorientated physically and mentally. Clare is Epping Forest's most eloquent and radical defender in the tradition of the poetry of complaint.

Epping Forest itself has a long literary history that interweaves with the use of woods in poetry. Elizabethan poets and courtiers, such as George Gascoigne, Thomas Lodge and Lady Mary Wroth (1587-1653), lived and wrote in the wood. Wroth was the first English woman to publish an original work of prose fiction, *Urania* (1621).[11] This work within the Sidney-Spenser school has a supplement of 103 sonnets and songs, 'Pamphilia to Amphilanthus', was the first English sonnet sequence published by a woman. Lady Mary was a patron to poets, such as Ben Jonson, who dedicated *The Alchemist* (1610) to her and George Chapman. Johnson's poem 'To Sir Robert Wroth' employs a different pastoral language to the Sidney-Spenser poets to place his subject.

Helen and Edward Thomas, whose first book was *The Woodland Life* (1897), settled at High Beech cottage from October 1915 until 1917, when Edward was stationed at Loughton Camp and studied Clare.[12] Thomas' poetry has echoes of Clare's especially in a poem like 'Home' with its suggestion of dwelling in a place where the birds and the narrator have one memory and the same relationship to the wood. It is one of Thomas' poems of course that so inspired the young Robert Frost. The narrator hears the birds and sees the April mist and is at one with the environment. "'Twas home; one nationality".[13]

Clare hated the enclosure acts that sequestered land from the peasantry and well knew the impact of enclosed commons, parks and woodland. William Cobbett, in his *Rural Rides* (1830), questioned for what and for whom are the deer kept in the New Forest and why should any man be transported for catching Forest game when it is public property? The Commissioners of Woods and Forests farmed hay and planted saplings for the deer out of public money until the 1851 Deer Removal Act. Deer were never fully removed and the New Forest remains one of the largest unenclosed forest areas in England with unified Commons rights going back to a 1698 statute. Its complex "rights of common" pre-exist Royal hunting law. In 2005 it became a National Park with the Forestry Commission retaining its powers to manage Crown land and the Verderers under the New Forest Acts. Protest issues around the Forest continue, as it is hard to make a living from such stringent laws in what is largely a wasteland. Of

Letter 16: Forests

recent poems on the New Forest, Jeremy Hooker's collaboration with the sculptor, Lee Grandjean, entitled *Their Silence a Language*, is more concerned with tree-images than the social and economic history and ecology of the Forest. Hooker uses the tree as a symbol with different usages and meaning as a means to achieve perception. It effectively links trees and woods with creativity but misses out on their impact upon community identity. His images are sparse and simple, employing some of the analogies between carving and use of poetic language suggested by Donald Davie in *Ezra Pound: Poet as Sculptor* (1965), but without penetrating far beyond a narrow range of awareness and perception. It is, though, original in being about the trees of one Forest. Sadly, though the book fails to negotiate the real relations of the Forest and centres on a limited imagism and basic mythology, as in 'Druid Song'.[14]

Clare's response to Epping Forest can be interestingly compared to Andrew Marvell's 'Upon Appleton House, To My Lord Fairfax' (1651), a poem that features the private wood of Lord Fairfax. Here the first-person narrator confers with the birds and trees and wants to be one with their lives and world (stanza 71); considers how his mind is made safe by the wood and the manner of his contemplation (stanza 76) and longs to be enslaved by its protective brambles and briars, invoking an image of crucifixion as the key to a spiritual life (stanza 77) and ultimately the ordered world of Fairfax's country house.[15]

Marvell's wood is quite distinct from John Milton's *Comus: A Mask Presented at Ludlow Castle 1634* (1645), which concerns a young woman, the Lady, who becomes lost in a wild wood (Haywood Forest) near Ludlow Castle, the home of Comus, a magician shepherd. Comus lives a life of sexual and sensual excess and attempts to seduce the Lady with "orient liquor". With the help of her Christian brothers and the earth Goddess, Sabrina the Nymph, her virtue remains intact. However, Comus is not beaten and runs away to continue his ways. Milton breaks the conventions of both the masque and the pastoral by allowing Comus to survive. The wood is traditionally the scene of disruptive disorder conquered by the forces of virtue usually represented by the monarch. Milton's ending is open and there is no recourse to any pastoral nostalgia. The idea of using the wood as a setting for evil is anti-pastoral and the work has a radical aspect that Blake recognised when he wrote that Milton was "of the Devil's party". John Kinsella's recent version of *Comus* has seized upon this and develops the anti-pastoral elements of the original and places it within a contemporary setting. Commissioned by the Cambridge University Marlowe Society to celebrate Milton's 400th birthday, Kinsella's *Comus* interacts with the original and brings out its environmental and sexual subtexts. His Comus is a genetic scientist who swallows Viagra and amphetamines. The Lady's chastity, as in the original, concerns the temperate use of nature and self-control. Kinsella's Comus is interfering with nature and is seriously out of control. Temperance in the original is the virtue that ethically preserves the wood and earth.

As in the original, it is Sabrina the Nymph who springs to the defence of the Lady, at the Attendant Spirit's request, against the unethical scientist, and sings: "where rushes and willows and osier grow / We can let things be," and declares that there is no need for "Effluent pipes or phone towers, / Fertilisers that bring algae / To choke ducks and fish".[16]

Here the Lady becomes an eco-warrior delineating and arguing against Comus' excessive tampering with and exploitation of nature. However, virtue is seen as an incomplete or pragmatic answer as the saving of wild place in the developed world is at the expense of another in the third world. The Attendant Spirit eulogises that "all this greenie poetry / won't mean you'll lose your luxuries. / Those of you who'd follow me, / remember the code word: LIBERTY… / virtue doesn't mean you / can't have your cake and eat it too."[17]

Kinsella thinks globally in his revitalisation of verse drama and draws attention to the need for local action. Reading Kinsella, I hear echoes of seventeenth-century environmental concerns in our present situation, the problems of deforestation, air pollution, draining of wetlands (a concern of the Levellers), overbuilding, toxic mining, maltreatment of outcasts, gypsies and animals, destruction of habitats and dispossession of the poor, and the need to sing of the earth's complaints and the need for wise and ethical cultivation. The wood is not merely a place of sanctuary, as in Marvell's 'Upon Appleton House', or of the testing of conflicting virtues and vices, but also of potential regeneration.

Letter 16: Forests

Notes

[1] Sourced at http://www.archive.org/details/turbervilesbooke00turb
[2] See Robert Pogue Harrison, *Forests: The Shadow of Civilisation* Chicago: Chicago University Press 1992 p.76
[3] E.P. Thompson, *Whigs and Hunters* London: Allen Lane 1975 pp28–29
[4] Eric Mottram, *Windsor Forest* Heaton: Pig Press 1979 p.7
[5] Ibid p. 8
[6] Ibid p. 1
[7] Eric Mottram, *A Book of Herne: 1975–1981* Colne: Arrowspire Press 1981
[8] Maurice Merleau-Ponty, *The Phenomenology of Perception* London: Routledge Kegan Paul 1996 p.194
[9] John Clare, *Selected Poetry and Prose* Eds. Merryn Williams and Raymond Williams London: Methuen 1986 p.165
[10] John Rodgers, *The English Woodland* London: Batsford 1941 p.34
[11] William Addison, *Epping Forest: Its Literary and Historical Associations* London: J. M. Dent 1945
[12] Ibid p. 227
[13] Edward Thomas, *Collected Poems* Oxford: Oxford University Press 1981 p.59
[14] Jeremy Hooker and Lee Grandjean, *Their Silence A Language* London: Enitharmon Press 1993 p.42
[15] Andrew Marvell, *Selected Poems* Manchester: Carcanet Press 1988 pp.83–85
[16] John Kinsella, *Comus: A Dialogic Mask* Todmorden: Arc 2008 p.64
[17] Ibid p.68

www.ingramcontent.com/pod-product-compliance
Lightning Source LLC
Chambersburg PA
CBHW031149160426
43193CB00008B/303